ABSINTHE

WORLD LITERATURE IN TRANSLATION

VIBRATE!

Resounding the Frequencies of Africana in Translation

Editors : Frieda Ekotto, Imani Cooper, Xiaoxi Zhang

I0247273

26

ABSINTHE: World Literature in Translation is published twice a year by the Department of Comparative Literature at the University of Michigan.

ABSINTHE: World Literature in Translation receives the generous support of the following schools, offices and programs at the University of Michigan: Rackham Graduate School, Office of the Vice Provost for Global and Engaged Education, International Institute, and the Department of Romance Languages and Literatures.

Typesetting and Design
William Kalvin, Delmas Typesetting. Ann Arbor, Michigan delmastype.com

Printed at McNaughton & Gunn. Saline, Michigan
ISBN: 978-1-60785-578-1
ISSN: 1543-8449

sites.lsa.umich.edu/absinthe
Follow us on Twitter: @AbsintheJournal

Unless otherwise noted, all contents copyright © 2019 *Absinthe: World Literature in Translation* and the Department of Comparative Literature, University of Michigan.

ABSINTHE
World Literature in Translation

Dwayne Hayes
Founding Editor

Silke-Maria Weineck
Editor-in-Chief

Yopie Prins
Chair of Comparative Literature
at the University of Michigan—Publisher

Judith Gray
Administrator

Elisabeth Fertig
Graham Liddell
Genta Nishku
Managing Editors

ABSINTHE 26

vii   Acknowledgements

1   Introduction

Kagayi Ngobi
11   *Oluzungu Lumbe, English Language Is Death!* | *No Speaking Vernacular*

Moses Kilolo
37   *Kimwana Kithini Nikyalika Kivinduni, An Immortal Precariat Goes into the Night*

Abdilatif Abdalla
59   *Kuno Kunena, Speaking Out* | *Telezi, Slipperiness* | *Kibaruwa, Casual Laborer* | *Ungapomoka, Although It Has Fallen*
Translated by Kelly Askew and Abdilatif Abdalla

Reem Bassiouney
71   "ف" رسالة الى السيد , *Letter to Mr. "F"* | بطاطس مقلية, *French Fries* | حتى الساعة السابعة, *Until Seven o'Clock*
Translated by Xiaoxi Zhang

Nyambura Mpesha
89   *M-Diag* | *Nani?, Who?*

Mukoma Wa Ngugi
95   *Kidane-Diva "Come See the Other Me,"* from We Sing the Tizita to Unbury Our Dead with Song

Frieda Ekotto
107   *L'Art de Regarder: Une Lettre de Frieda Ekotto à Frida Khalo, The art of looking: A letter to Frida Kahlo from Frieda Ekotto*
Translated by Emily Goedde

Susan Kiguli

123 *Omuti, The Tree | Nnakazzadde, Mother | Wayirindi, The Plague | The Unending Game, Omuzannyo Ogutakoma*
Translated by Merit Kabugo

Afua Ansong

135 ⊛ ⏳ ✳
"The Earth Is Heavy/Holds Weight" | "Drum"
"Ananse's Web"

Mary Pena

141 *Rescripting Visual Codes: A Poetic Translation*

Elizabeth Mputu

153 *Charcoal Toothpaste*

Imani Cooper Mkandawire

165 *Inheritance, Ode to N'TOO*

175 Contributors

Acknowledgements

The editorial team of *Vibrate!* would like to express great appreciation to the Department of Afroamerican and African Studies and the Centre for African Studies for their generous donation to this issue of *Absinthe*. We also wish to thank Kelly Askew, Stephanie Bosch Santana, and Simon Gikandi for advising us towards your networks of brilliant translators, writers, and scholars. Uhuru Phalafala, we value the time you spent conceptualizing *Vibrate!* in its initial phases. Your expansive and imaginative understanding of Africanity in translation was inspirational. Thank you Emily Goedde for reading our translations. And thank you to everyone who shared our spirit, and who have been supporting us generously in other, yet equally important ways.

This is for you.

Introduction

The idea for this journal issue began with an interest in publishing works written in "local languages" in Africa, because when we talk about African literature today, we mostly are concerned with African authors who write in European languages (English, French, German, Portuguese, Italian and Spanish). Since African literature and its aesthetics are also translations of European languages, it is important to return to seminal works such as Ngũgĩ wa Thiong'o *Decolonising the Mind: The Politics of Language in African Literature* (1986) and Aimé Césaire's *Discourse on Colonialism* (1950). These texts analyze the struggle for language in Africans' right to humanity. For wa Thiong'o, the call for the rediscovery and the revalorization of African languages remains a process of decolonizing history. The new way to think about African history is to re-read it or to take it to new expanses. For Césaire, colonial discourse dehumanizes the African, hence the need to seize oneself as a historical subject, for it is through language that one transmits culture. The key question then becomes: What culture are we transmitting right now?

We have contributions in colonial languages including French and English because we fundamentally believe that these languages are African languages. The Chadian writer Nimrod calls for the need to make French an African language. In *La Nouvelle Chose française*, he writes: "it is time we consider French an African language."[1] Since it is impossible to write in Dùala, her mother tongue, Frieda Ekotto decided to write her piece in her colonial language as a process of decolonization.

Perhaps it is time we expand translation theory to discuss African literature. An African writer's imagination moves from creolized languages and cultures to a European language. In this sense, we cannot talk about African literature without translation. We need

---

[1]Nimrod. *La Nouvelle Chose française*. Arles: Actes Sud, 2008. p. 27.

to reconceptualize the notion of "translation" while acknowledging that European languages have already become a venue for African expressions.

It is hard, if not impossible, to engage with the question of language in African literature without a critical sense of the impact of European colonialism on the continent.

Many consider the "Scramble for Africa" that followed the now infamous Berlin Conference in 1884–85 to be the culmination of European colonialism in the continent. While in 1870, only around ten percent of the African territory was formally under the control of the Europeans, in less than half a century, by 1914, only ten percent of the territory remained in the hands of the Africans. However, such a view presumes a totalizing perspective toward the continent from the outside, which often alienates one from the concrete daily experiences of colonialism associated with the continent.

Indeed, due to the arbitrariness of colonial division of the continent, and the varied experiences and practices of the Europeans in the African continent across centuries, people from different geographical areas or historical moments have varied experiences of "colonialism." In the realm of linguistic practice, although it is known that the colonial policy of indirect rule, adopted by the British and the Germans, and the corresponding linguistic practice of adaptation varied drastically from the policies of the French and the Portuguese, who preferred a more direct approach that imposes the languages of the colonizers as the only recognized official language in public domains and formal practices. It should be highlighted that the degree of implementation of their policies also varied significantly from region to region and in different historical periods, both as a result of domestic resistance of culturally and socially distinct local communities and as a result of the shift of immediate interests of the colonial metropolises.

Take the example of Kiswahili. Despite being recognized as a compelling example of an African language, one cannot take for granted the indigeneity of the language to its users in the continent without also considering the arbitrary employment of the language by the German and British colonizers for regional administrative purposes. Resistance to the use of the language was registered whenever the regulated use of the Swahili language implicated inequality and subordination to an imposed social hierarchy, which constituted a dynamic factor the colonial government had to consider in the evaluation of its language policy. When the colonial government no longer invested heavily in the Swahili language and decided to encourage direct use of a European language, Swahili was also voluntarily taken up by many speakers who, despite their varied relationships with the language, made use of it due to its status as a regional lingua franca for effective communication in the midst of anti-imperial struggles.

The history of the standardization and the promotion of Swahili under colonial governments also engenders a coerced separation between Arabic and the African continent, or at least between a limited profile of the "Arabic language" and part of the African continent, as it was created in the minds of the colonizers. If, in the case of the Swahili-speaking regions, "de-arabization" and the forced adoption of the Latin script can be understood as a noble gesture of the restoration of an authentic "Bantu" culture free from the contamination of the external forces of the Arabs, such an interpretation would hardly sound reasonable if one takes into account the various Arabic-speaking communities in the continent, and the fact that they were all negatively affected by European imperialism and still suffer from the consequences of it. The various layers of experiences of "colonialism," which also go together with different kinds of policies, on the other hand, call for an expanded understanding of colonialism capable of accommodating the miscellaneous oppressive experiences that forcefully tied a whole continent together.

It is crucial to understand the impact of colonialism for a critical appreciation of works written in African languages, not because European civilization succeeded in reshaping the African continent according to its own interests, but because in every possible moment, the Africans were always readily disposed to turn the imposed cultural elements into weapons of resistance, to the extent that any non-historical affirmation of the cultural identity of a language *as* being "African" runs the risk of falling into a problematic trap of authenticity that bears imperial connotations alienated from reality experienced in Africa. To this effect, Chidi Amuta, in *The Theory of*

African Literature, calls for a more comprehensive understanding of the question of language in African literature to effectively carry the revolutionary spirit and ideological pursuits of everyone from the continent who advocated the use of local languages as an anticolonial gesture:

> Literary creativity and consumption in each African country is simultaneously taking place in both the European and African languages. While the bulk of oral literary creativity is being carried out in African languages in the rural areas, much of written literature is done in European languages. African literature written in English, French, and Portuguese exists alongside a growing tradition of written literature in Yoruba, Igbo, Gikuyu and Xosa. Given this spectacle, to insist that African literature be created exclusively in either of these sets of languages is to ignore the social and historical predication of the language situation itself. Even if all of African literature were suddenly to be created in African language without due attention to the ideological content of the literature and its relationship with its audience, the revolutionary dreams of the advocates of linguistic indigenization would be thwarted.
>
> If literature *qua* literature is to play its sectoral role as a cultural force in the transformation of society, then the language question needs to be redefined in more pragmatic terms. The problem, to my mind, is not that of language in the sense of verbal signification—that is, European vs. African—but rather that of strategies for cultural communication in a neo-colonial situation. In effect, language needs to be reconceptualized to mean the totality of the *means* available for communicating a cultural form to the greatest majority in a manner that will achieve a clearly defined cognitive–ideological effect in the consciousness of the audience so defined. [. . .]
>
> Language *qua* language is therefore not the issue in African literature. The problem of communication in our literature is directly related to the forces that prevent human communica-

tion at the economic and social levels. As part of the struggle to correct this anomaly, all the avenues of cultural communication should be explored to get the benefit of progressive revolutionary literature across to the greatest possible majority of our peoples. In this respect, European languages, African languages, oral performance, written expression, radio broadcasts, etc. are implicated.[2]

In other words, the "language question" in African literature inevitably entails the procedure of bridging the gap between socio-economic development in the post-colonial era, which still demands heavy use of European languages for practical purposes, and dignified cultural recognition free from the oppressive burdens of colonialism. At the same time, productive discussions about the language of African literature should also serve as the hub of communications for anti-imperial endeavors in every sense at different levels.

This understanding also leads to a renewed understanding of the place of a translation. In his famous essay "Des Tours de Babel," Jacques Derrida calls into question the hierarchy between the original and the translation and draws attention to the quality of both the original and the translation within each individual context. In African contexts, translation from or into a local tongue is often predicated upon one's sensitivity to the socio-historical conditions that shape one's understanding of language, as well as an active attempt towards liberation. The translation, on the other hand, should also be read as a hybrid cultural and social rendering of the spirit of the original drawn from "all the avenues of cultural communication" for the sake of cross-cultural transcendence and liberation, instead of a word-for-word rendering from an "original" based on a conventional linguistic or stylistic framework.

In addition to reading for the stylistic challenges towards the notion of a language per se and the limitations of a specific genre as understood by many, it is also worth mentioning that there are more than fifty recognized countries in Africa, and among which no less than twenty-four countries take English as their official language for

---

[2]Amuta, Chidi. *The Theory of African Literature*. London: Zed Books, 1989. p. 112.

various reasons. In addition, there is also a big population of African descent living in the diaspora, among whom many have English or another non-African local language either as their first language, or as a language of substantial importance in different capacities. Even if what we are able to cover in this issue is only a very small part of the literary and artistic productions related to language and Africa, we are still feeling short of space to do justice to the context each specific piece entails. Therefore, we invite the readers to read imaginatively, and also to look for the reason and the value of the linguistic varieties associated to the use of one single language, as well as the relationship between the writer and a language.

Outside of language-based notions of translation, and recognized in the *Oxford English Dictionary*, translation also denotes "the expression or rendering of something in another medium or form."[3] The Chicago School of Media Theory considers how language- and non-language-based modes of translation can be understood in relation, specifically how each "offer different orientations of a similar process: the first describing a change of form within a medium, viz. language; while the latter describes a process that is enacted between media."[4] However, this issue of *Absinthe* considers yet another definition of translation, one that encompasses both intra-medium and inter-media processes: translation defined as "transformation, movement, shift."[5] Though this lateral definition has fallen out of common use, much of African and black diasporic theory, art, and literature is informed by a complex politics of forced and volitional transformation through European colonialism, not just in language, but in land, and the construction of self.

In contemporary Congolese artist Sammy Baloji's *Mémoire*,[6] black bodies haunt the frame, wavering between gray and gossamer, charcoal and opaque. In this multimedia photography series,

---

[3]"art, n.1." OED Online. Oxford University Press, June 2019. Web. 23 July 2019
[4]Lund, Karsten. "The Chicago School of Media Theory Theorizing Media since 2003." The Chicago School of Media Theory RSS, 2007, lucian.uchicago.edu/blogs/mediatheory/keywords/translation/.
[5]"art, n.1." OED Online. Oxford University Press, June 2019. Web. 23 July 2019
[6]*Mémoire* can be translated in English to mean the literary genre of memoir writing. It can also mean memory, remembrance or keeping something in mind.

Baloji juxtaposes archival images from 1906 of European officials and Congolese laborers who worked for the Belgian mining company, Mining Union of the Upper Katanga (now Gécamines), with original photographs taken 100 years later. Though the images overlay a century, they evoke iterations of industrial yet barren landscapes, ashen and vexed laborers, and uneven power relations. Through photography Baloji affords a kind of time travel and critical reflection on how European colonial practices of exploitation continue inhuman conditions in the mines. Baloji allows us to perceive how colonial greed translates into the Congolese landscape. However, there are multiple registers of translation in motion. While the images transpose time, the photographs themselves are acts of translation through the medium (digital photographs overlay archival images on satin matte paper). As such, it is worth considering the multiple layers of translation at play within Africa and its diasporas that transcend the verbal.

It is in this spirit Vibrate! contemplates the implications of Africa and its diasporas in translation, moving through temporalities and mediums, from the literary to mixed media, and pivots on a notion of translation generated by particular modes of questioning identity, and various colonial histories that engender underlying assumptions about blackness.

This issue is robust with contradictions exhibiting linguistic, geographical, and conceptual tensions, contending with what it means to speak from various kinds of African and African diasporic identities. While some contributors highlight the frustrations of expressing Africanity through colonial languages, others consider colonial languages possible vernaculars with which to challenge colonial thought, using both colonial and local African languages with intention. Still, some insist on promoting the enriching qualities of local African languages like Yoruba. And some contributors turn to various forms of code and media as a method to consider the poetics of translating blackness and Africanity.

An ethical reading and appreciation of literature written by African writers, or art works put together by African artists, in a Western space demands genuine intellectual and practical efforts to discard the colonial relics that obstinately survive into the current moment, in pursuit of a better future of prosperity that does not have to rest upon exploitation, subordination and elimination of other people. It is therefore convenient to quote from two verses[7] written by the renowned Mozambican woman writer Paulina Chiziane's *The Song of the Slaves*,[8] composed to honor the slaves and other "offspring of Africa" who suffered the consequences of imperialism, and to facilitate remembrance of the essence of African literature and culture:

Africanidade[9]
A africanidade não está na superficialidade garrida das capulanas
Africanidade é a busca da tua existência desde o princípio do mundo
É libertar a mente para não te colonizares a ti mesmo
É colocar o saber das academias ao serviço da liberdade
Africanity
Africanity is not in the smug superficiality of capulanas
Africanity is the search of your existence from the beginning of the world
It is to liberate the mind so that you do not colonize yourself
It is to put the knowledge of the academies at the service of liberty

Frieda Ekotto, Imani Cooper Mkandawire and Xiaoxi Zhang

---

[7]In the epigraph, Paulina Chiziane did not call this work poetry. Instead she wrote,

Com estes versos escravos, remontamos à raiz de todos os conflitos.
São versos livres, tristes, alegres, musicados, para ritmar a dança da história.

[With these slave verses, we reassemble the root of all the conflicts.
[These verses are free, sad, happy, musical, to give rhythm to the dance of the history.]
[8]O Canto dos Escravos, Maputo: Matiko e Arte, Lda, 2017.
[9]The part quoted in this introduction is only one stanza of the entire poetic song. It is translated by Xiaoxi Zhang.

Untitled 2016 | Njabulo Dzonzi

Kagayi Ngobi

Oluzungu lumbe, English Language Is Death! | *No Speaking Vernacular*

Translated by the author

OLUZUNGU LUMBE[1] (Lusoga)

Oluzungu lumbe!
                Lwise abaana be nsi eno-
Oluzungu lumbe!
                Lutusibye amajegere-
                          Oluzungu lulimi lukawa inho-
                                Luliku na magha-
Luwanda busagwa-
                Oluzungu lumbe!
Oluzungu lumbe!
                              Lututwaire abaana baife-
Lututwaire amagezi gaife-
                Lutukwese ebyobugaiga-
Nga ebyobuwangwa byaife-
                Oluzungu lumbe!
Oluzungu lumbe!
              Batukuba gya nte-
                      Okwega olulimi olwo-
                            Olulimi olutali lwaiffe-
Batukoba edhaiffe-
         Mbu dhiri 'local'-
Obuntubulamu buweire wo-
                            Lufuire abosomi kizibu eri ensi yaife-
                Oluzungu lumbe!
                Oluzungu lumbe!

---

[1] This poem was written in Lusoga and translated into English.

ENGLISH LANGUAGE IS DEATH!

English language is death!
   It has killed the children of this world—
English language is death!
     It has chained us—
       English language is a bitter tongue!
         It has thorns all over it—
It spits poison—
    English language is death!
English language is death!
         It has taken our children away—
      It has taken away our knowledge—
     It has hidden our treasures—
Like our cultures—
    English language is death!
English language is death!
      They beat us like cows—
        To learn this language—
          To learn not of our people—
They tell us of our own—
    That they are 'local'—
Our humanness is used up—
      It has turned the learners into a problem to our country—
       English language is death!
     English language!

NO SPEAKING VERNACULAR![2] (WOLOOLO)

FOR YOU
GRACE DAMBYA

AND THE REST OF US
PUNISHED AT SCHOOL
FOR SPEAKING

OUR MOTHER TONGUES.

---

[2] This poem was written in English and is meant to appear only in English.

1
Aha! It's you Dambya

Today I have caught you!
Today you are not escaping me!
Dambya, I have heard you
Today I have heard you
With my own ears
You have said GWE

Get out get out
Get out of the dorm
Come outside here
You let him pass
Come, come, come
Every day, every single day,
They report to me
That you use vernacular
And every time I ask you
You deny, you say they lie,
And you can deny, Dambya—
You are so good at denying
But today I have caught you
With my own ears!

I have heard you
Speaking vernacular
Today no denying!
Today no?

But Dambya, why? Why
Do you always speak vernacular
And you deny?
Dambya why are you so local?
What do you not know?
The school rules and regulations?

Who allowed you
To speak your mother tongue?

Dambya, if you cannot talk English
How will you learn?
If you cannot talk English
How will you pass?
If you cannot talk English
How will you communicate?
If you cannot talk English
Where will you get a job
In the future?

The reason your parents
Brought you to this school
Is so that we transplant
The village out of you
And make you civilized

You have to speak English
All the time, all the?

Excuse me! Yes, you!
Run to the staff room
You know where I sit?
Check under my desk there
You will see my stick
You know it, not so?
Bring it to me
Hurry I don't have time

Dambya, the reason
I am going to give you
15 strokes of that cane
Is not because I am a bad person
No, it is because I want to remove
That village out of you

That is why your parents
Brought you to this school

Lie down, ah, ah
Sorry for what?
Dambya if I do not cane you
You will not understand
Dambya no bargaining
No, no
Sorry for what?
Ah! Ah!

Dambya lie down
Sorry for what?
Dambya no, no
No negotiating

Today I caught you
With my own?

Lie down.

Dambya, you know
The school rules, not so?
No speaking vernacular
Full stop.

Aha! This is the stick
I was talking about
As flexible as I like it!
Dambya you know
What it is up next, not so?
'Sugar Special Time'

Hehehe! Go down
You touch there
I don't count.

✦ ✦ ✦

2
Good morning school

The teacher on duty
Has already talked about it
The Speech Prefect
Has also talked about it
Last week I also touched on it
But once again, I shall emphasize it:
The issue of vernacular
Being used in this school
Should be put to bed
Once and for all, full stop.

Vernacular speaking
In this school
Should stop.

It is a problem now
Becoming a disease!

Local languages
Belong in your village homes
Not among the civilized here

In this school we only allow you
To speak foreign languages
Local languages are forbidden
Local languages are?
The school rules are clear!
All of you must know
This is not a local school.

Now yesterday I caught this boy,
Where is he? Where is Dambya?

Come now in front here
For the whole school to see
The village in you; where is he?
Aha! This one. You boy
You are very stubborn, kneel down!

School, you all know this boy,
Look at him

This boy is very stubborn
Every day they report to me this Dambya
That he uses vernacular
But when he is caught, ho!
He becomes a problem;
He threatens prefects
That him he cannot be touched
Because him he is big

But yesterday was the day
I was doing inspection
I saw Dambya seated there in his dorm
One slipper blue, another one red
Am I lying?
I heard him tell his friend GWE

I heard him with my own ears

So this week — the sisal sack
And bone necklace
Belong to Dambya of S.5
'The Early Man of the Week'
You are to wear them today
From morning up to end of class
To serve the example to others
Like you out there who think
This school is for the uncivilized and local
We are a first class school

And we speak English
We speak?

Now you stand up —
Get that thing and wear it now
Also put on that necklace
Today you are going
To stand outside my office
Until school ends
To demonstrate to the other Dambyas
Out there who may be tempted
To think we are not serious
On this language issue

We are very serious

Today you will not eat break or lunch
You will only wait for evening porridge
And you will be the last to be served

School I hope this serves
As a warning to all of you

As the administration
We are committed
To being a first class school
That is good in English
That is good in?

From today onwards,
No Speaking Vernacular in this School.
Repeat after me:
No Speaking Vernacular in this School
(No Speaking Vernacular in this School)
Tell your neighbor
No speaking vernacular in our School
(No speaking vernacular in our School)

Alright, have a great week.

3
Good morning teachers

Thank you teacher-on-duty
For those remarks
I am glad dorm inspection
Was done in no time

I also want to thank
All those teachers who marked
And handed in all their results
That is the spirit
We must be showing
Because this year our theme
Is Team No Sleep

I do not expect
Any teacher to sleep
Until this school beams
As the modem of
Modernity on this village

Dear teachers, we must not sleep
Our ears must not sleep—
To bring modernity
To this school permanently
We must fight this growing disease
Of vernacular speaking conclusively
And we must fight it together
We must fight it?

But, but, teachers
I am not at ease
It has come to my attention

Some of you do not cooperate
At giving the sisal sack
And bone necklace
To vernacular speakers in your class;
It is a shame some of you also
Communicate in vernacular
With students imagine!

Dear teachers
Unless you want to know
Why a dog has no horns,
Why are some of you
Stupid to that level?

How can a teacher and a student
Have the same brain?

This language issue
Is going to get some people
In this room fired if they think
This is a joking subject

For example this boy Dambya
Who I caught myself (MYSELF!)
I caught him saying GWE

But to get him I had to get out
All my tactics; I tiptoed like this
Like this, like this,
Up to behind his dormitory
I was there for thirty minutes
Waiting to catch him
But finally I did. I did!

How come none of you
Managed to capture him before?
I suspect some of you teachers

Have been covering him
Because he is a common culprit

Now I will use him
For the whole school to know
How a head filled with local languages
(Like one rotten tomato)
Should never contaminate
The heads of our students

I don't want that.
I don't want local languages
To infest my school like Nairobi flies

I am going to call
Dambya's parents
To come and we end
This issue: either he leaves
His local languages home
Or he leaves this school
Once and for all full stop.

As I conclude teachers
Our target this year
Is to score very highly
In the national exams
And what does that mean?

No spreading vernacular because
Exams are set in English

That is my message
For this particular week
Those of you sleeping, wake up
Please teachers remember
To call Dambya to stand
In your class as an example

Of what this school should not be
Whenever possible.

Have a great week.

4
Good morning class

Ready for literature?

Do I have to repeat
What the headmaster repeated
After what I repeated here last week?

You heard the headmaster again—
On assembly
No more vernacular speaking
So from today onwards
If I hear any vernacular

You will face the music
Of that boy Dambya

So make my work easy
By speaking only English
And in this literature class it even
Makes my work easily easier

The good thing is
English is an international language
It can make you travel
But local languages
They take you where?
To your villages
Is that where you want to end up?

You see the books we teach
In what language are they?
In what language is the national anthem?
In what language is the national motto?
In what language is the national constitution?

So make my work easy
By speaking only English
And in this literature class it even
Makes my work easily easier

Where did we stop last time?
Where did we stop?
Where did we stop last time?
All of you open your books
And put your novels on top of your desks
You, you do not have the novel?
You, you left it in dorm?
Yours, a friend borrowed it?
All of you go and lie down there

Now you ki-girl, you also
Do not have the novel?
Do not waste my time
Just go in front there
And lie flat, your forehead
On the floor, and stay there

What kind students are you
Who come to my literature class
Without the novel?
Can you go to the garden
Without your hoe?

Class, I say this all the time
If you want to pass this subject
What do you do?

Carry your book to
Copy your notes to
Sharpen your tongue to
Pronounce your pronouns and
Sing your syntax as
The heart palpitates to
The pace of the plot thru
The pentameter and
Just like that,
You are civilized!

You, who likes Ateso, look at you
Can you make such rhyme
Without reading book?
Can you even make that
In your mother tongue?

Is there even literature
In your mother tongue?

Literature is literature
Only in English

You people without books
What do we do for you?
I don't want empty tins in my class

Without books
You are empty tins

Go to the D.O.S.
Tell him to choose for you
another subject
I don't want you in mine
I am paid to teach students
Not empty tins

Now this ki-girl crying
Without books
How can you study literature?
Literature is in books
And if you don't have books
You don't belong to this class!

Out!

5
Daudi

Kumbe you are Dambya's uncle?

You said his parents live far?
And even now
They are not in the country?

That is okay
Come to my office

We wanted to *only* talk to his father
Because this issue at hand
Is very serious

But, Daudi, since I know you
For old times' sake
I shall speak to you

This Dambya you see was caught
Speaking vernacular
By no one else except myself

I caught him this time
With my own ears

It is a very serious issue
It means Dambya shall not
Pass his exams
It will be bad for the school
And we do not want that here

Daudi, we have already
Decided Dambya deserves
An exemplary punishment
A suspension of three weeks
To serve as a reminder
To him and the others
Who speak vernacular

It is irregular

Daudi, this son of yours
Is very stubborn
He even teases my prefects
But this time

I caught him with my own ears
Daudi this issue is very serious

He said GWE
In the dormitory
And I was there

Take him home
And let him he speak
All the local languages he wants
When he returns I want to see him
Immunized from vernacular
Ready to speak only English

No, Daudi, no, please do not plead
Do not kneel,

God, this is disgusting
Daudi the decision is final
Daudi it cannot be changed

He threatens my prefects!

Take Dambya with you
Dambya you must learn
To respect our regulations
I want my school
To be a first class school

Now, if you excuse me
Daudi take your son with you
And bring him back after three weeks

I hope he learns
His lesson this time

English is the language
Of the civilized.

6
Excuse me, give me ko your pen

Eh eh you, that is vernacular

Sha! We are not in class
Those things stop at the school ends

Education is also practiced after school

Sha! School is school
Dorm is dorm
Market is market
And a garden is a garden

Take your lugezigezi
Back to your headmaster!

Eh eh, you; Mr. Full Stop says
He has ears all over the place
What if he hears you talking now?

Akole ki? You fear fear a lot you also

Without English
You will fail your exams

Look here
Even teachers are teachers
Because they failed the exams
Of lifestyle and lifetime

Teachers are failures?

Eeeh! Teachers are failures
Who take their failures
Out on us by being mean
Because they see us
As the dreams they will never be

Me I fear being beaten like Dambya

Imagine being there
And all you think of is
How to use pain
Umbu to bring success
Kyoka carrying around a cane
As if military police!

But without English

There is no job for you

Mpa ku pen naawe
I want to beat this ffene
But I cannot reach it.

You, you don't fear
Being beaten like Dambya?

Dambya kyali wange
Oyo Mr. Full Stop talina magezi
Education is not about what you teach
But what I observe
And I observe this ffene is ripe
Bring the pen

We will keep some for Dambya?

Of course man we have to!
Mwana boyi ali mu kawunyemu
This school is fake
It needs to give me a break

It has also reached my neck

Get your neck out of the way
I am bringing down the ffene

I hear they are calling Dambya's zei's
Kale for just one word
GWE

Kwata pen yo
You have homework to do
Not so?
Nanti you fear

Being beaten like Dambya
Not so?
Get your pen
With the masanda
Let it stick to your hands
All the time
To make Mr. Full Stop happy.

I hate that man
Dambya did nothing wrong

Dambya did nothing. Full Stop.

✦ ✦ ✦

7
Early man! Early man!

DAMBYA WELCOME BACK!

Early man! Early man!

Early man Dambya!

Dambya welcome back!

Story ki Dambya? Mwana what's up?

Man you missed the kadanke

And the interact func

Man you missed the Rugger game

Man how was home?

Hi, Dambya

Hiiii Dambya

This Dambya is back

You Dambya, come here
So you are back?

Early man Dambya!

Today is Friday
I hope you have all
All your class notes by Monday
If you don't you will know
Why a dog has no horns

Dambya, you stubborn boy!
Come here. Carry these books
To the staffroom

Hahahaha! So you are back Dambya?

DAMBYADAMBYADAMBYA

Lie down I cane you

How was home?

Did you speak enough vernacular

In your Lusoga?

I hope you learnt your lesson

You looked good in the sack

And that necklace too!

I wish we catch you another time!
Alright you go to class
The bell for the next lesson already went

Dambya! DAMBYA! DAMBYA!

Chief Vernacular speaker!
Zinjathropus poster!

Enter class Dambya, but keep
Your local languages outside!
Do not spread them in here DO YOU HEAR?

(Excuse, is that the one
Mr. Full Stop called Stupid Boy?)
-He is the one-

That one he will fail exams
He will be a failure in life
That one he will fail exams
He hates English

What's up Dambya?

The village boy!

Hahahaha! The village boy!
Hahahahaha!

Dambya what's wrong?
Come on man stop being angry
We are only joking

Man, stop catching feelings
Man me I'm your buddy
Dambya, this is a small issue

Just be cool
Ignore everyone
I know this school is fake man

But you will make it through.

✦ ✦ ✦

Moses Kilolo

Kimwana Kithini Nikyalika Kivinduni, An Immortal Precariat Goes into the Night

Translated by the author

Kimwana Kithini Nikyalika Kivinduni[1]

Elliot esima tiivii na ayulwa ni stalehee syakwe mituki, ayiungama kuma sovasetini nikana asome SMS simuni. Awĩnja niwamuandikia nikana mathi makatembee. Ĩndĩ eiwa woo mwingi nunduwa mechaniki uthukukumaa na kelele mwingi vakuvi na vala wikalaa Roysambu, vau utee wa lelu munene wa Thika. Nundu ndatony'a kumwika undu, eũma makaniki usu ngooni, aũmanitye maeyo na esilitwe mesilwa maingi. Simu yake ya Samsung Galaxy yiĩwa yi ngĩto muno yila wesilwa yiulu wa Mũlatwa na wasya wake wi mwololo muno. Namo moko make na syaa mausie yuũtia yila yiutuma kioo kya simu kiyithiwa kikwatene. Lakini nundu ena wendi munene, emantha namba ila sivwaa ta swina wikwatyo wikavaa. Kuma yila wookie Ilovĩ niwamanyĩie kwitasya silingi ngili imwe. Amĩtaa K, ndeto ya Sheng ila umitumĩia muno ayienda kuvoya mbesa.

Eĩwa wĩa mwingi ki, ta isatani yiũmwĩta ngingo eesilwa kumukunia simu Mũlatwa. Nĩ wĩa utaawiwa ona aitembea stlĩtini sya Ilovĩ eweka utuku kati, ayenda kwiwa ta ve vandu vaseo wita musyi. Mithenya mingi ewaa emenete vyũ. Mũno mũno yila ũendaa maũfisini maingi kumantha wia na andũ asũ maimwia tũ atie mathangũ make ma kumina sũkũlũ. Ĩndĩ masaa ma utuku vyu wiwaa amendete mũno, yila musyi munene wa Ilovĩ wikalaa ta ukomete. Masaani asũ no andu anini methiawa leluni: ala matakomaa, athukumi anoũ kĩ ma maufisi matwaite gali syoo nene sya Toyota na Mercedes maĩmantha kwendwa, twilitu twikĩite tukula tukuvi vyũ, na ĩndĩ syokola. Onthe maimantha kwiwa o nesa kiwiyooni mateusumbuwa ni mũndũ. No askali tũ mamakĩiaa maikakwate ni musako. Ona ou wiovo, Elliot aitembea Ilovĩ masaa asũ ma utuku ateũkia kindu ona kimwe. Lakini yũ ayenda kumukunia Mũlatwa simu eiwa vinya wonthe uimuthela. Esindwa vyu kivinyiia kambaton kau ka girini kumukunia simu mwanake umwitaa mwanaa iya.

Elliot etina kavakũli mwou yila ukuũngama kuma kisovasetini athi kisũmbani cha ukoma. Nũndũ ndekwenda kuthamba eona tũ evake marashi ma aũme ala metawa Yardley Legacy. Kamunthyũngo kau kaseo niko kindu chai cha mbee Awĩnja wamwendeĩe. Mũthen-

---

[1] This story is written in Kamba, a popular spoken Bantu language in Kenya.

ya usu Awĩnja amwonie aungamite nza wa mbaa yitawaa Gipsy, aikunda kundanga vangĩ. O vau tenange mũthenyani ousu we Elliot niwatetanisye na mbosi wake ula waleea kumuandika kwawo onaethiwa niwamuthukumite mwei muonza ila meewanite. Vangĩ ũsũ ni wamutetheeasya ndakethiwe na meswilya maito muno.

Nake Awĩnja anywĩtwe ũkĩ mwingi ukatũmaa ayelũka, ayumya <u>mũnyũngo</u> mũthũkũ mũno. Oyĩla mũnyungo ũsu wathelĩle ona mayaa ona kana vai na thina ona vanini. Awĩnja amuvalukiĩla Elliot ta maĩ anyanya ma kuma tene. Nake Elliot eewa kamũyo kaingi nundu wa kukoomewa ni nondo isu nene swa Awĩnja kithũĩni kyake, Awĩnja amwiĩlile matau ngingoni na moko make makwatĩĩle ĩtũo syake o sekondi nini. Na maĩvakũvĩ kuvalukanya yĩla Awĩnja watangatangie. Elliot niwamũkwatĩe na mitũkĩ na kwoko kwake kwa aũme kwekalanga o vaũ yĩũlũ wa kitimba kwake kinoũ kiseo, na kĩkonde mũongonĩ kyai kyololo nesa. Kwa ndatĩka oĩmwe, metho moo nimakomanĩe vau mamũlĩkitwe ni kyeni cha nza cha mbaa ĩsũ yeetawaa Gipsy. Navo vau mokoni make Awĩnja niweewĩe kaundu kaseo. Metho make asũ maĩ ma mbraũnĩ makwatwa ni methoĩ. Ĩndĩ Elliot niwaleile kwitikila kana methoi asu maĩ ma wendo. Metho ma Awĩnja ona mayaakomwa ni ũnywĩ, makanite tamamwene mbee wa mwĩĩ wake ngĩnya nthĩni ngooni.

Awĩnja ndaaeka kumusyaĩĩsya utuku usu ona yĩla mekalile vau nza ya golofa isu yai utee wa mbaa. Nĩvo Awĩnja wamanthie sikala muvukoni wake kwa mĩtuki mĩtuki. Elliot nake ndaa ananga ndakĩka, oosa kĩlĩvĩtĩ amukwatisya. Awinja aendeĩe kũmũsuva, nake asyoka na ĩtĩna nikana aũngame nesa. Nĩvo ĩndĩ Awĩnja wakũndĩe kasikala kaũ na aathamya nikana syuki yukile yo mbeene ateũyilasimithwa. Na ĩndĩ Awinja akũna sĩmĩtĩ ĩkovĩ oĩnini, ayenda Elliot oke kwikala vakuvi nake. Mekalite vaũ Elliot niwasiisye oona ivisi na elĩĩtu maitembea makwatene moko, angi ala manywite muno makwatĩlĩĩlwe maĩkavalũke. Na vaĩ o elĩtũ elĩ kakonani vandũ maendee na kũmũmũnyana, na vakũvĩ namo kĩvĩsĩ cha yĩika yake kwaũmanaa simũni. Ni wekalile vakũvĩ na Awĩnja, ũla nake waĩlĩile manyũũ make satĩni yake, akunda munyung'o wa marashi. Nĩvo Awĩnja weewĩe muyo na asisya kungi, muvaka ĩvu ya Elliot yeekũnza. Ila wamanyie kana ndenekee niwookililye kituo kwake na anyungĩa makwava make.

Ĩndĩ Awĩnja amusiswa na amũkulwa: "We nũe ũũ?"

Nake asũngia: "Elliot."

"Elliot? Wimanisha Elliot ta ũla waandikaa voemu?"

"Ayiee, ta mwĩni wa mbathi sya kisasa sya Amelika. Nye kondaumite kuya New York, na ni vaa Ilovĩ tu mweĩ o nini, na ĩndĩ Njanuary ndisyoka kuya Amelika."

O athekete vanini, Awĩnja asya: "Winyung'a nesa, Elliot."

Ĩndi kwivaka marashi ni kindu George wa Mũlatwa woona ta wana, tĩ kĩndũ cha ndũme take. Mũlatwa avũthitye tabia ĩsũ vyũ, oundũ ũtendete kukengana. Noo uvũngu nawo Elliot niwawendete muno. Nicho woonie kunyunga nesa kwi kuseo kũvĩta kũneena ũwo yĩla mundu wina mwendwa wake.

Ethĩ mbavũ na ayĩũngama nthĩ ya kĩwũ kivyu cha kĩthambio, avũngĩte metho na vĩnya aeke kwisilwa ĩũlũ wa Mũlatwa. We eenda mesilwa ala memuyo ma matũkũ ala maseo na Awĩnja, yĩla wathukumaa vengi ya utuĩnĩ. Mavinda asu athukumie tu mwaĩ ĩtatũ na avũtwa nũndũ wĩa niwathelile. Ĩndi maũandiki aa ma ĩvalũa kũya vengini, kampuni site swa silikali, na ũsomĩnĩ maũndu asũ ma ĩvalũa ni mamwiwithisye woo muno.

Kĩwũ kĩmwĩtikĩĩa na kumũnya savũnĩ mituki. Ona ndanakĩĩta mũongo kana maaũ atanambakuma kithambĩonĩ. Nasyo ngũa eisyikia mĩtũkĩ, ekiite itĩĩshati yiasa yiendanye na njiins swake sya langi wa matu. Ĩndĩ kĩndũ kila kimwaĩlite vyu ni ĩatũ. Niwaendia ndukani nene swa Mr. Price na Avilas aimantha ĩatũ nzaũ sya matuku aya. Lakini nawo kila wakatano nuamukaa tene vyũ athi syoko ya Kĩkomba matũka kuũ matanavunguwa. Kuthoowa mutumba museo wa kisasa tĩ vinya wavika tene. Elliot muno muno niwisi kumantha na e vaati nzeo. Lakini niwiwaa ve vĩnya aĩmũelesya Awĩnja nduka ila kuya Westlands wathooĩe kiatu kyu. Ũmunthi ekiĩte kĩatũ cha nduka ya Ataliano yitawa Salvatore Ferragamo. Etata muno kutumia gluũ kikwatanyithwa maandiko ma kĩatũ nundu nimekumakumanga. Naĩndĩ yinthangu yiĩtilika aĩendee na kuyilasimithya. We tĩ mundu wa kwika maundu nesa, na eona vala ithangu yũ yiandikitwe isyitwa ya brandi ĩsũ yiumwanangia saa sywake. Ayivaka marashi aũngamite mbee wa kĩoo, na munyung'o ũsũ museo nĩ ta ngua nyololo imwilingite.

Aũmaalũka nyumba eĩsila kasilani kala kakwatanitwe Roysambu ya tene na ila ĩnaakiwe oyu. Eona tũ ve mundu wĩsĩ kila ngaliko ya kasilani kau ka TRM. Lakini vaĩ umwe ukũungama kumukethya nũndũ ena halaka. Nyumba ĩsũ nene ya kuthooa syĩndu yĩo ndakĩka ĩtano kuma kwake, na kila ĩtambya yimuetete vakũvĩ na George Mũlatwa.

Elĩkĩila TRM kwĩsĩla mũoma wa ĩtĩna. Andũ aĩngi vyũ nimekalite vau va kuthooa leũ, maĩneena na wasya muninĩ. Vamĩlĩa na endani onthe maendee kumanthana na kwendana maiya leũ sya muthemba wonthe. Mbaa nene yitawaa Persia ndinandũ yũ nũndũ ni muthenya, lakini wĩyoo yĩthĩawa na andu aĩngĩ maiya laha. Golofanĩ ya keelĩ ya nyumba ĩno yĩ na matuka maĩngĩ, lakini ndekwendeesya yũ ni ndũka ya kuta syĩndũ sya mathaũ kana ĩla ya kuta syĩndũ sya kompũta ya Apple. Veo ivinda wendete ndũka ĩsũ muno. Eenda tũ kumwona Mulatya uvisini wake, ula ni kakivanda kanĩnĩ kethiawa vau katikati wa matuka. Mulatya emwona na aithingithya mũtwe wake kumyonya nĩwamwona. Atanamba kumuneenya ekeuka kusisya muthooĩ wake ũla ũkwenda kaseti ya kivindi cha Game of Thrones. Uthyu wa Mulatya uũsia kyeni yila ũkusmĩli lakini mataũ make manoũ mavyaa ta mavakĩtwe maũta maĩngi kĩ. Eĩtu eli maũngamite o vaũ maĩsyisya mavuku ma sinema nikana mathooe, na nomeũvinduka ĩmwe kwa ĩmwe mamutheche Elliot.

Ĩndĩ mwĩsyo Mulatya nukukeuka amusisye Elliot, na ayiendeea kuneena ta eusomaa musoa.

"Nye niniamue kumantha mbesa nikana nongeleele nduka ĩno yakwa. Ikonomi ya Kenya nĩyithi naku. Nye niĩka undu nitonya, na nienda yu we undĩve kila niunengete nundu nikuma tene naukovethya."

"Wienda kumbanya mbesa siana?"

"Ngĩlĩ maana atatu. Ve nduka nzeo muno vaa maisye yiithiwa yi nthei mwei uũ ukite na nienda kumyosa nikana none biashara ĩi yakwa itonya kuthi va."

O yila simu yake yaĩa Elliot nukulikana na kyeva kingi kana niwamutavitye Mulatya yiulu wa wia wa mbesa mbingi unakwatite vau mwei uyambiia. Amwie wia ũsũ akwatie kumana na anyanya ma ĩthe wake ma biashara.

Simu niyakunwa ingi, na amisisya Elliot eona ani Awĩnja

ũkũnite. Alea kumyosa simu ĩsũ namo mamessenji melika kulika. Awĩnja emwia kana kethiwa ndeuka we eona nukuthi na anyanyawa make kundu kungi makasherehekee kusyawa kwa umwe woo.

"We, Mulatya, nĩenda unenge o ngĩlĩ ĩtano o mituki mituku ninguutungia mbosi wakwa ambiva matuku miongo ĩlĩ na nthyanthya. Ona ni na mbesa ingi niteele o vandu matuku o asũ. Ninguũsoti mani."

"Yaani mwanoo wienda ngunenge ngĩlĩ ĩtano oyũ oyũ?"

Yu Mulatya kouteulea na vinya na kuneena na wasya mwingi nginya eitũ asũ matindie masyitwe ĩatũ sya Elliot mamusisya ũthyũ.

"Yaani mwanoo ona inya wakwa ndakwata silingi imwe kuma kwakwa yũ. Nganenga mundu kindu omunthenya ula biashara ĩĩ ngwetwe yooka sawa sawa. Niĩkwatwa nuelewa yu kimwana, na no wisi kana wĩ na ngili sykwa ikumi na itano."

Elliot ena woo mwingi kwiwa undu Mulatya ukwisilwa, nginya akaumana:

"Ngĩti!"

Ena woo usu wonthe Elliot ayumaaluka matukani asũ ateunjali Mulatya na andu onthe ala wakomana namo measya ata.

Ĩla woosa simu amukunie Peter, nivo ukwona kana o na nde na klenditi. Lakini Safaricom nayo ndimunengaa 'please call me' na ko unatumia syonthe. Kooũ ayasya asanda kwa matu na nthi kwa kumunenga syama on nini nini. We na Peter nimesene vyũ kibiashala, na niwisi kana ndetindwa thinani ũũ wa mukwata yu.

Peter aimwosa na kumutwaa kula Awĩnja wikalaa. Ĩndĩ we Elliot ailea kuthi kumwosa nyumba, aimukunia simu oke nthi.

Nake Awĩnja aĩmwia:

"Nenge o ndakika ĩmwe kindu chakwa. Nitukite."

Elliot na Peter meetelile vakuvi na ndakika miongo ina na itano, na nivo Elliot watumiĩe ivinda yĩu kutata kumwia Peter antheeanje mbesa ila wendaa kuivya. Ĩndĩ ndeto ĩsũ niswamwiwithisye woo mwingi muno Peter, nũndu mamwĩite eteele na Elliot nowendaa aninivyange mbesa. Ĩndĩ mwiso Peter niweetikilile kuivwa ngĩlĩ itatu kethiwa nimaekanie nake athi mawiani angi na aimosa mamina kunywa uki woo. Ona ve ũũ Peter niwaisye nilasima aivye nusu, na nusu ila ingi ayiivya amenukywa.

Awĩnja aumaluka ookie na Caro, mwĩitu munyanyae Elliot

wamwonete o imwe vaũ mbeange. Namo kotemeekiite tusulwali twoonanitwe matako moo vyu. Nichokitumi imwana syaungamite nza wa nduka ya Samu maekie kuneena na mamasũviliila tu. Onasyo iveti ila syaumite kuthooa mboka nosyavindukie kwona eitũ asũ. Ĩatũ ila ndaasa Awĩnja weekite syauitwe ni asyai make mekalaa muiongo kuya Paris, Kivalanza. Namo ni asyai umonaa o imwe kwa mwaka. Ona ve uũ niwendete aĩtu ĩsu, lakini nisya mulasimithisya kutembea o mbola. Ĩndĩ mwiso avika ngalini evũngũa muomo kwa mituki Elliot atanamba kivikia kwika oũ.

Eĩtu asũ eli ona mayaaea ngewa ya maana na Elliot. Ĩndĩ kati woo nimaneenie muno uilu wa tivi na ivindi ila meloelaa. Oimwe kwa imwe Awĩnja nowe wamukulalya Elliot kana niweetikila undu waasasya. Lakini Elliot ndendete ngewa ĩsu maneenaa yiulu wa eĩtu mendate maundu ma ĩndanetĩ na maisha ma yiulu muno. We asisya o vanini vau ivila sya itina eitu mekalite, na niwoonie kana Caro niwamusimiaa metho, ayukilya maau make o vanini ta ukumwia Elliot ni asisye uthei wake. Ndakika o ikumi siithela mai mavikie Mountain Mall. Eĩtu mauma ngalini we Elliot atiwa vaũ aineena na Peter. Ĩtĩna wa ndikika o ĩli niwamaatĩĩe na malika liftini nikana mathi kilavu cheetawa Comfort golofani ya katatu. Makwatie ivila vakuvi na kiwanza kya kusunga vai vakuvi na mbaa.

Weita amina kumakulya mendaa kunywa chau Elliot niwamuatĩĩa na kumutyetya muno, na eĩtũ nimeuseng'a nichau kĩendee vau. Ona yila wasyoka vala maĩ simu yake yitindia kuia. Ayienda maikone oũ, Elliot emitiliila vau muvukoni, lakini nake Awĩnja ula oona nichau kieendee aimyosa kwa mituki muno.

"Itila yii! Niki uteosa simu ya ndeleva wa taksii?"

Ve kuseng'a kwigi mbee wa woo wasyani wake Awĩnja. Nivo Elliot ukumea mamweteele o vanini athi kuneenya Peter vala umutiie. Yuyu ona Peter niwumie ngalini aungama nza, ekiite ivulana ya grini yiutuma ayikala ta imwana inene ya sukulu.

Ena woo mwingi Peter aimwia:

"Nienda mbesa syakwa oyuyu na ndukone ta uũndindya vaa. Nina wia wa kwika."

"Tuliza mboli naku Peter. Tuliza."

Onakau vayai mundu wi vakuvi kumewa, Elliot emukwata Peter kwoko na kumutwaa ovau kando maneene. Metetanwa muno, Elliot aneenete Kikamba kiito kiutuma Peter ayisilya notamaumite o vandu vamwe kuya utuini.

Ĩndĩ Peter ayisa kwasya: "Nye ninguelewa kimwana, lakini, konisa kuungama vaa wiyoo wonthe nikweteele nandunandiva."

"Nisawa ĩndĩ tutwae kuya Westalands ngakuivie vo. ATM ya vaa ndiuthukama."

Awĩnja ndeenda kumwa kiwanzani cha usunga. Elliot amukwata kwoko ekukukuna amueke. Esunga na ĩmundu ĩnoũ yina kitambi kinene, na kwoko kwake Awĩnja kukwatiie ngusu ya itina ya mundu usu, vala vena woleti noũ vyũ. Awĩnja kukuna kwoko kwa Elliot aeke kumukwata, o yila ĩmundu yĩu yiumuthengeea Awĩnja matuni nikana yimusuviliile kaundu. Nivo mwiso Elliot amukusya na vinya mathi nza. Awĩnja aisemba kwosa ũkĩ wake na kuvuvuutya. Nivo ĩndĩ aĩthingithya mutwe wake ta mundu ukwatwite ni majini. Elliot aĩmwia Caro amutwae Awĩnja ngalini, nundu vau itina ve weita umuatiie. Vala mavika nza memweteela vakuvi ndakika miongo ili.

Nivo ĩndĩ Awinja ukumukwata kwoko na vinya na kumukulwa:

"Nichau kieendee ĩndĩ? Ndavye oyu kana nikume?"

Indi Elliot aimusunguia:

"Tuendete kuya Westlands nikwo kwi maundu maseo mbee wa kuu."

Mavika Westlands emea eĩtũ asu mamweteele kilavuni cha Aqua. We Caro ethi imwe kwa imwe kusunga, atingithitye kitimba ta elitu ala ma vindio sya musiki tiiviini maisunga wathi wa Njaman njuisi. Nake Awĩnja ayikala kwa aeini ma ndaia na kwitwa isovi. Elliot e nza aineena na Peter ula yu wambiie kukita na askari ma muomoni ayenda kulika.

"We, we, aume, ekanai nake uũ ni ndeleva wakwa wa taksii, ninguneena nake."

Masonga utee Elliot ayambiia kuneena na ka aksendi ka Amelika, o undu MuAmerika mwiu utonya kuneena. Lakini Peter nake ndeenda kwiwa utumanu ũsu, ndeto syake sya Kikamba siteuma nesa nundu wa woo. Elliot aimwosa kumutwaa vau utee, lakini nake Peter koukwenda kwiwa kĩndu ona vanini.

"Ithukiisyi Peter, naku ithukiisye Peter niki? Ninguunenga simu yakwa alafu uindũngia uni nakũiva, sawa? Sawa Peter?"

"Ati simu? Simu yaki nye ko ngwenda simu yaku. Nienda undive mbesa swakwa ndia ĩno. Koona ta nisa kulwa kana chumwa kithelu ndwaandiva ona ndululu imwe."

"Kino. Peter. Kino."

"Ndukaumane we ndia iĩ. Ndukatate kuũmania vaa."

"Ĩndĩ naku Peter ni chau yũ nanotwisene? Simu ii ngũunenga ni ya ngili miongo ina na kenda, yaani wiisilwa . . ."

"Miete."

Peter aĩmyosa simu ĩsu na mituki na kuthi taksiini yake. Elliot einguma ovu amusyaiisye. Ĩndĩ avinduka eona Awĩnja auingaminte itina wake, aumanitwe maeyo na woo mwingi kĩ. Nake Caro eo vu itina wa Awĩnja, aumukomba.

Awĩnja nake aimukulwa Elliot:

"Ni chau kieendee?"

"Vai kindu, nisawa vyu." Elliot aimusungia. "Kwani ko mwaeka kunywa?"

"Weita ni watuetee mbilu yitu, asya ndeenda kwiwa kana nue ukuiva. Yaani mwanoo ukaa mbaa na uĩnywa na klenditi na nduivaa?"

"Klenditi kiva we?"

"Ndia ino nuu ula withiawa ena mandeni kilavuni?"

"Tuliza mboli Awĩnja, nilasima weita usu ndesi kila ukuweta."

"Sawa. Aya yu ndavie, niki Peter wathi, na tena athi na simu yaku?"

"Ĩthukiisye ngutavye kendu wakwa, sawa, ĩthukiisye ngutavye ũwo. Nyie ndinakwata mbesa umunthi ila ngwonaa ta ngukwata."

Awĩnja ayambiia kuthi, ateenda kwiwa oũ. Onakau alevi aingi nimambiisya kumasyaiisya, Elliot we ndakwete oũ woo. Ayosa kwoko kwa Awĩnja nikana amwisuve.

Awinja aimwia:

"Nienda kwinuka nye, mbitie taksii."

"Nionaa twambe kwosa matatu kuma vaa nginya taoni alafu kuma vau tuyosa taksii nginya kwaku? Ĩi, wiona ata kendu wakwa?"

"Nye, yu? Yaani ko wimutumanu ata? Wiona tanikiie ngua ta ii nikana nilike matatuni?"

Elliot esisya kuu na kuya, on imwe aimwia Caro amutetheesye. Lakini nake Caro ndeenda ou wake. Ona kula kumusimia metho nikuthelile. Eĩtu asu me eli mayienda kuneena nake ona vanini.

Nundu wa aivu Elliot ayiungamya taksii yambee kumyona, na onthe mailika mituki. Mavika leluni munene wa Thika ngali isu iyosa spidi nene muno. Nivo ĩndĩ Elliot aisonga vakuvi na Awĩnja.

"Naku mwendwa wakwa mbelewe tu. Niendaa wone kana ninikwendete."

"Yaani wiendaa kwithiwa wi ngũmbaũ, ee?"

Elliot aimukomeea kithui na kwambiia kũĩa o mbola. Awĩnja nake ayiwa tei, amukwata mutwe na kumunweenwa na kawasya kaseo. Nake ndeleva wa taksii ndananeena ona ndeto imwe. Kethiwa ena wia wa kulea kuivwa ni alevi asu ndiowananwa ona vanini. Ona yila mavika Roysambu ndeuweta kindu, nayu Elliot ayambiia kwiwa wĩa mwingi nundu ndesi ndeleva ũsu atonya kwika ata. Ona no kava ala maneenaa na mawasya manene mayenda kuivwa. Ila Elliot woona ndeleva usu ayosa kindu ungu wa kivila chake ngoo yake ikunite kukuna. Veo ngewa weewie yiulu wa ndeleva sya taksii syithiawa na pastola siitumiaa kuyia andu. Yu vaa ko mayaina kindu oteo thayu syoo.

Ĩndĩ ndeleva usu aimea:

"Osai namba yakwa na muindiva uni."

Nivo vau onthe meewa matetheka muno. Ona utuku usu wekala ta weeuva. Yũ Elliot akwata kĩnyunyu kya Awĩnja mwiitu usu ona ndaamuvata. Maitiana na ndeleva usu mewite o muyo mwingi. Caro nake aimea makome nesa na kuthi vala wikalaa. Nivo ĩndĩ Elliot na Awĩnja maithi nyũmba makwatene moko.

"Kiwiyoo kii kumbe no kikwisaa usauva?" Elliot amwia Awĩnja.

"Tui tuisane o nesa nikana tulwe ni maundu asu mathuku."

Mavika nyumba Awĩnja elika kithambioni mituki. Auma kuthamba emwithia Elliot eyovete taweli ila yake ingi. Nivo ĩndĩ ukuthi akamukuna kakisi matauni na aimwia:

"Enda wambe kuthamba."

Nake Elliot aimusungia: "Nivo vau yu kendu wakwa."

Ethamba mituki muno, ota undu wikaa yila uteuthamba vamye na Awĩnja. Ona ndanakua ndakika itano. Aumaaluka eithia muomo wa nyumba ya ukoma wa Awĩnja wi muvinge. Navau kisovasetini ve ivula ya kwivyika. Emukunangia Awĩnja muomo, yambee ombola mbola, ĩndĩ Awĩnja alea kuvungua nukukuna na vinya muno. Awĩnja aelea vyu kuvungua. Na ĩndĩ Elliot ayikala vau kivilani mbee wa isaa yimwe, aimwisuva Awĩnja avungue lakini Awĩnja ndeitika ona imwe. Lakini Elliot noukumwiwa kindu wake vau nthini. Mala nukukooa, lakini muno muno eneena nai na kumana, ngiti iĩ!

Mwiso nukuma nyumba saa nyanya sya utuku, itina wa kuya masilingi Awĩnja eeite kavalukini vau vakuvi na tiivii. Elika matatuni itena abilia ona umwe, lakini yiendete tauni. Ngali isu kawaida ikuaa andu ikumi na ana. Lakini nao makunite musiki wina wasya mwingi ki, uutuma kelele isu iyananga kukilwa kwa kiwiyoo kiu.

Niivo ĩndĩ ukumiswa Ilovĩ taoni nthini kula ukwiwa thayu wake ta ukwitwa ni mandaimoni. Etembea mituki mituki athengee eitu ala maungamite laini vau stlitini wa Koinange. Evungua metho make muno, ayona kana amalasimthwa kuvunguka ou nukumwona mwiitu wa inya ula witawa Aggy. Ni Aggy eweka umulilikanasya undu mundu wiwaa kwithiwa na usyaaniwa, ona kethiwa ndaila kumwona mwaka mingi muno. Na ngoo yake yina thina mwingi. Namo mesilwa ni maito ki. Nivo ayiwa wasya ndu ya ivuti, na indi *swwiiii* wa kisasi yiathite kungi. Ĩndĩ o mituki ayiwa ivuti yingi yamuatha kituoni, yikamulasimithya kutulya ndu, vakuvi avaluke nthi vyu. Ivisa yake ya mwiso kuyona ni ya Aggy, auite mbu nene na asembete kuka vala ũĩ. Ndesa kumanya Aggy amusembeete na muyo kumwona kana ni woo wa kila cheekika. Na o mbola mbola ayona kiwiyoo kĩi kiyusua kĩvindu kinene na kukilwa vyu, na ayiyiwa avalukite vandu vololo veumumelwa tene na tene.

An Immortal Precariat Goes into the Night

Elliot mutes the television and forgets the comfort of his couch as he sits up to read Awinja's message, inviting him to take her out. He wants to scream at the arc welder next to his Roysambu flat along Thika Road, but lets out a silent and bitter curse instead, his thoughts racing. His Samsung Galaxy Trend feels heavier when he thinks of Mulatwa's soft-spoken voice. His sweaty palms and fingers make the touch screen sticky. But he scrolls on and on, looking for promising contacts. It seems he has called almost everyone in the past month, except Aggy, his sister. Always asking for a K, a letter he has become too fond of, for the ease with which he can say it when he needs money.[2]

When Elliot wants to call Mulatwa on the phone, fear becomes a devil suffocating his daring soul. He feels no fear when he takes his solitary, nocturnal walks in the streets of Nairobi in search of something to call home. His days are clouded with thick self-loathing, having knocked on office doors in and out of town and handed out copies of international business qualification papers. His favorite hours begin when the city seems engulfed in a strange sense of sleep—when only the insomniacs, the love-desperate, the pot-bellied office-holders driving Toyotas and Mercedes dominate the streets along with half-naked girls and homeless boys and girls. Each seek their piece of nightly space and freedom, interrupted only on occasion by Askaris on patrol. Fear never shows up at such moments. But he is paralyzed when he goes to press a button, a simple green button, to call a man he calls brother.

Elliot rises from the couch and knocks over an ashtray as he makes his way to the bedroom. He considers just changing clothes and spraying himself with a bottle of Yardley Legacy for Men. The fragrance is the first thing Awinja noticed about him.

She walked up to him on a Friday night when he stood alone outside Gipsy Bar, smoking a joint. Earlier that day, he had an altercation with a boss who would not confirm him for a permanent

---

[2]The use of K here is slightly borrowed from Sheng. K in Nairobi Lingo is used specifically to refer to a thousand shillings (approximately 10 USD), as one would use the word grand or G in American slang.

position after seven months, and he turned to his joint because the puffs helped create a universe where everything seemed laughable. Except there was nothing to laugh about in Awinja's two belches that night, enveloping them in rotten breath. But after a few seconds of disgust neither seemed to care. She just slumped herself on him like an old friend. And he relished the soft feeling of her rather large breasts on his chest, her chin on his neck as her hands wrapped around his neck for a few seconds, and then slipped away as she fell backwards. He reached quickly for her and with his right hand, held her tightly just above her exposed waistline, a soft curvature of flesh, smooth skin. For a single moment their eyes met under that colored glow of Gipsy Bar's security lights. In his hands she felt delicate. Her big brown eyes seemed wet, but he dismissed the thought that she'd been crying. Not dimmed by her drunkenness, they shone bright as though they could see past his physical elements and into his soul.

Awinja did not take her eyes off him that night as they sat on the next building's entrance stairs and she fumbled in her bag for a cigarette, which he quickly offered to light. For a while her facial expressions didn't change, she stared at him, even as his dark face retreated and his body regained an upright posture. Finally she took a long puff and let the smoke rise from her mouth without effort. She motioned for him to sit, slapping the stairs rather crudely with her right palm. He looked around and saw boys and girls walking hand in hand, some propping each other up because alcohol was fast immobilizing them. In a corner two girls were kissing, and a boy about his age was cursing on the phone. He sat. And she brought her nose closer to his shirt, took a full, brief inhale that took in his mild cologne. She smiled and looked away, making him tuck in the muscles of his abdomen. Discreetly, he lifted his left shoulder close to his nose an' breathed in deep.

"Who are you?" she asked.

"Elliot," he said.

"Elliot? Like Eliot the poet?"

"More like an aspiring rapper. I'm from New York, visiting Nairobi for a few months, and then I'll go back by January."

"You smell nice, Elliot!" she said.

George Mulatwa thought adorning oneself with cologne was

childish, not sexy. He despised it perhaps as much as lying, a trait that came to Elliot almost naturally. But to smell and feel fresh in the company of his lover was more important than any truth that could bind Elliot to his brother.

He goes into the shower and stands beneath the warm water, eyes shut to block out Mulatwa's face. He wants to think only of the better days with Awinja, when he had a stint at a local bank, when he had worked for a three-month contract until they said they were no longer hiring. A few contracts later in banks, NGOs, academia, the word "contract" became something he mentioned bitterly.

The falling water quickly washes the lather from his body, and he barely scrubs his back or even his feet before jumping out of the shower. He dresses quickly, wearing a long white T-shirt with his faded blue jeans. His signature is his shoes. He has been to Mr. Price and Avilas in search of the latest fashion. But on the first Friday of every month he wakes up at five in the morning to make sure to be at the Gikomba market before the stalls open. A haven for copycats, it's never hard to find something fancy and new. And Elliot has always been lucky, although he sometimes finds it hard to explain to Awinja the particular shop in Westlands where he gets each pair. Today he chooses something from Salvatore Ferragamo Italia. He tries to stick the loose label back on with super glue, but the paper tears. He is too impatient to join the two halves correctly, so he just leaves them. He stands before the mirror and sprays his armpits, only lightly, so the cologne falls like a soft cloak around him.

He takes the path that connects the old Roysambu with the new. On each side of the TRM Drive, he sees someone he knows, but he does not stop to catch up, even though he feels he should. The mall being only a five-minute walk from his house, every step he takes draws him closer to George Mulatwa.

He goes into the mall via the back entrance. To his right, a low hum hangs over the food court, teeming with families and lovers cementing their living bonds over choice foods. The Persia Bar and Sheesha Lounge are empty for now, as if carefully preserving themselves for the life-giving night. On the second floor are a variety of shops, but neither the Sports House nor the Elite Digital, which sells the most expensive Apple products, interest him as they once did. He just needs to see Mulatwa in his *office*, and he walks straight to the third stall in the hallway. Mulatwa sees him and nods, but then turns immediately to a customer, demanding to know whether the sixth season of *Game of Thrones* is out. Mulatwa always wears a smile that brightens his face and makes his flabby cheeks seem oily. Two girls flip through booklets of printed posters and make their orders. Every now and then they turn and smile at Elliot.

Mulatwa turns finally to Elliot and addresses him as if continuing a monologue he was already having in his head.

"I have decided to raise some money to expand this business. Fuck corporate Kenya. I will do my own shit. And I am counting on you, bro. Pay me what you owe me now, it's been too long, bro."

"What are you looking to raise?"

"Three hundred thousand. I got a very good deal with a larger shop that will be vacant in the mall by next month. Man, so much space to explore what this business can become. And you have my fifteen K."

"But I told you about my job situation, Mulatwa."

Just as his phone rings, Elliot remembers with a deep sense of sadness and confusion that he'd told Mulatwa about a new six-figure salaried job he had gotten earlier in the month from some business associates of his father.

The phone rings again. Awinja. He does not answer and texts follow almost immediately. If he can't make it in an hour, she might go with her girlfriends to a birthday party out of town.

"Look, Mulatwa, I need 5K urgently. My boss will pay me by the twenty-eighth and all my other money will mature by the twenty-eighth as well. I will sort you out, man."

"You want me to give you 5K? Now?"

Mulatwa shakes his head and raises his voice, and the girls who had been looking at Elliot's shoes look up at his face.

"Nah man, no no. Not even my mother is getting a cent 'til my business deal goes through. You understand now, don't you? And my 15 thousand you have."

"Fuck!" Elliot curses under his breath.

He walks away fast, not caring about anything that Mulatwa is saying behind him, or even the giggles he thinks are coming from every face he meets.

He calls Peter, his cab guy, only to realize he does not have credit on his phone. He is fortunate to have one more chance to use Safaricom's Okoa Jahazi service. Thank the universe for small miracles. He and Peter have done business on many occasions, and Elliot is confident about navigating the crisis.

He does not go up when Peter parks outside Awinja's house.

"Honey," Elliot says when he calls her on the phone, "I'm downstairs."

"Just a minute, sweetheart! We'll be out in a bit."

For close to forty-five minutes, Elliot negotiates a fair price to keep Peter there.

But each passing minute seems to make Peter angrier, unwilling to be kept waiting even as he keeps negotiating the price. Finally he settles for three thousand, but he will leave to do other runs and pick them up when they are done drinking. Elliot is eager to agree. Half now, half later is what Peter wants. Period.

When she walks out into the cold breeze dressed in hot pants, Awinja is accompanied by Carol, a friend Elliot has seen only once before. A few boys seated outside Sam's Shop stop talking and stare. Heads turn even among the women who are returning from the mama mboga. Awinja wears high heels brought in from Paris by her parents whom she sees once every few years. She walks with long but steady footsteps, opening the door for herself before Elliot can do it.

Their conversation in the car barely involves Elliot, except for the occasional "Don't you think so, honey?" from Awinja. They analyze and overanalyze television, and all the latest misadventures by the town socialites. Elliot glances at the back seat once in a while, and Carol always seems to wink at him, raising her leg rather slowly as if daring him to look in between. In ten minutes they are at the Mountain Mall. Elliot lingers, and speaks to Peter for a while. They take the lift to Club Comfort on the third floor, and sit at a table close to the dance floor.

Elliot stands to follow the waiter who has taken their orders, in a conversation that seems both longer and more heated than necessary. When he sits down his phone won't stop ringing. He fumbles in his pockets and disconnects the calls. Awinja grabs it.

"What the fuck? Why are you not picking the cabbie's call?"

There is more surprise than anger in her voice. Elliot excuses himself and goes downstairs to Peter. Still wearing his green sweater that makes him look like an overgrown high school kid, Peter stands outside his car.

"I want my money now. And don't keep me waiting; I have work to do."

"Calm down Peter. Calm down."

Elliot takes his hand and leads him aside, even though there is no one else around who would overhear them. They have a long conversation, Elliot spewing words in unadulterated Kikamba. Peter thinks that they may be from the same village even.

"I understand you," Peter says finally, "but I have to work and I can't stand here waiting for you all night."

"Okay, take us to Westlands. I will give you all your money for the night there. The ATM here is not working."

Awinja shakes off his hand when Elliot tries to lead her off the dance floor. She almost clings to the pot-bellied man she is dancing with, her hand roving into his back pocket, stuffed with a huge wallet. The man whispers in her ear, and she smiles each time, pushing Elliot behind her. But as they walk out she takes a long sip of her drink and shakes her head. The waiter is still trailing Elliot with the bill, so he asks Carol to lead Awinja out. He joins them almost twenty minutes later.

"What is going on, Elliot?" Awinja screams. "What is this mysterious bullshit you are giving us? Ah?"

She grabs his hand.

"Talk to me. Okay. Tell me what the fuck is going on."

"We are going to Westlands, okay. It's better fun there."

In Westlands the girls are asked to wait upstairs in the Aqua Club. Carol jumps on the dance floor and begins to shake her bum, imitating the video vixens on the TV screens, doing it to "German Juice." Awinja sits in the VIP section and orders a glass of red wine. Elliot goes back downstairs to talk to Peter, who is pushing his way past the bouncers at the door.

"Yo, what's up guys? This here is my cab guy. Let me sort him out."

Elliot speaks with a practiced accent, a pathetic copy of American gangster rappers. But Peter is shouting at him now. His Kikuyu words are distorted by anger, and even when Elliot takes him aside he does not quiet down.

"Look, look, Peter. Look, I will give you my phone, and then you can return it to me when I pay you tomorrow. Okay?"

"Phone. I don't want your phone. I want my money, you fool. You want me to forget that last month you did not pay me for a whole week straight?"

"Fuck. Peter. Fuck."

"Don't curse me you empty-headed fool."

"Peter. You know me now. This phone I am giving you is worth forty-nine thousand.

"You think . . ."

"Bring it."

Peter grabs it and walks to the taxi. Elliot does not move for a minute. When he turns Awinja is standing there looking at him, frozen with anger. Carol is behind Awinja, making faces.

"What's going on?" Awinja asks.

"Nothing. Nothing." Elliot's voice is almost shaking. "Why are you not upstairs drinking?"

"The waiter brought the bill. She says she does not want to hear that you are the one paying. You have a debt from last week and the week before."

"A debt?"

"Who the fuck has a debt in a night club?"

"Hey, there is some confusion here."

"Alright. Why has Peter left? And why did he take your phone with him?"

"Listen, babe. Listen. I just didn't come into the cash I was hoping for."

Awinja starts to walk away. Elliot follows, trying to hold her hand and not caring much for revelers that have started to snoop.

"I want to go home." Awinja says. "Please get me a cab!"

"I was thinking we should first take a matatu to town, and then from there we will get a cab to your place."

"Me? On a matatu? You think I dressed like this so that I can get into a matatu?"

Elliot's eyes rove all over the place. He turns to Carol for help, but the girl does not wink or smile at him anymore. Neither girl wants to talk to him, so he waves down the first cab he sees and they all get in. As they cruise down Forest Road to the super highway Elliot reaches out to Awinja.

"Please honey, just understand. I wanted to make you see that I love you."

"You wanted to be a hero? Yes?"

Elliot leans into her chest and he begins to sob slowly. A sigh escapes Awinja, who takes his head against her and calms her voice. The cab driver says nothing. If he is worried about the possibility of unpaid labor he does not show it. When they arrive, he does not say anything either. Elliot is more worried by this than noisy demands. When he reaches for something beneath the seat, Elliot feels his heartbeat rise. He once heard rumors of a taxi driver who had a gun in his car and stole his clients' belongings. Here, they have nothing but their lives.

"Take my number," the taxi driver says, "and pay me tomorrow."

There is a collective sigh of relief. The night brightens, and Awinja does not move away when Elliot places his hand around her waist. They part with the taxi driver with an elated mood they don't believe they deserve, and as Carol walks towards her flat alone, Elliot holds Awinja's hand.

"The night has finally gotten better." Elliot says. "Let's have fun and forget all this shit."

Awinja gets into the shower immediately after they step into the house. When she comes back to her room, she finds Elliot wrapped in the spare towel. She walks up to him and gives him a peck.

"Why don't you take a shower first," she says.

"Alright, my love."

He showers too fast, like he always does when he is not sharing it with her. In five minutes he is done. He finds her bedroom door locked. He can see a blanket has been thrown on the couch. He knocks on the door, slowly at first, but receiving no reply, he knocks harder.

She does not answer. He sits there outside of her bedroom for an hour, begging for her to open, and not once does she answer. But he can hear her inside. Sometimes she sneezes, sometimes she screams.

Fuck!

He walks out of the house at two in the morning, with the coins from the jar that sits beside the TV. He gets into a matatu going to town, the only other passenger in the fourteen-seater with music so loud it feels like a violation to the sanctity of the night.

He is dropped in the heart of a city whose caged demons suffocate his soul. And he walks faster and faster towards the girls that line Koinange Street, his eyes bulging as though the wider he opens them the easier it will be to see Aggy among them, the fading memory of his only blood relation. And as his heart sinks deeper into the abyss, his ears are shut temporarily by the shrill, initial swish of a stray bullet, and then the penetrating pain of another through his right shoulder, driving him to his knees. His last image is of Aggy, running towards him screaming. With joy or pain he does not know. And then slowly the night grows so dark and quiet he feels himself fall into a soft, swallowing infinity.

Abdilatif Abdalla

Kuno Kunena, Speaking Out | *Telezi*, Slipperiness | *Kibaruwa*, Casual Laborer | *Ungapomoka*, Although It Has Fallen

Translated by **Kelly Askew** *and* **Abdilatif Abdalla**

Kuno Kunena

Kuno kunena kwa nini, kukanikomeya kuno?
Kwani kunena kunani, kukashikwa kani vino?
Kani iso na kiini, na kuninuniya mno
Kanama nako kunena, kwaonekana ni kuwi

Kana na kuku kunena, kunenwa kakutakiwi
Kuna wanakokuona, kunena kwamba si kuwi
Kunena wakikuona, kukuita kawakawi
Kunena kana kwanuka, nikukome kukunena?

  - *19 Julai 1970*

Speaking Out

Why has speaking out provoked my imprisonment?
What therein compelled my confinement?
Invalid insistence incited anger against me
Apparently speaking out is viewed with contempt

Speaking out may be distasteful to some
Yet others do not regard it negatively
Encountering each other, they hesitate not to embrace
So if speaking out stinks, should I shut up?

  – *30 October 2014, Ann Arbor, MI*

Telezi

1
Mvuwa iliyonyesha, ya maradi na ngurumo
Kutwa na kucha kukesha, kunyesha pasi kipimo
Haikuwanufaisha, wenye kazi za vilimo
Wenye kazi za vilimo, walifikwa na hasara
2
Mimeya waloipanda, ilitekukatekuka
Kazi ngumu walotenda, yote ikaharibika
Hawakuvuna matunda, waliyo wakiyataka
Waliyo wakiyataka, yakawa ya mbali nao
3
Wenye kuicha mvuwa, isiwatose mwilini
Baadhi yao wakawa, wakimbiliya penuni
Wengine hawakutuwa, hadi mwao majumbani
Hadi mwao majumbani, na kukomeya milango
4
Wenzangu dhihaka kando, nisemayo ni yakini
Ilibwaga kubwa shindo, mvuwa hiyo jamani
Na mijaji kwa mikondo, yakawa barabarani
Yakawa barabarani, mvuwa kwisha kunyesha
5
Kunyesha iliposiya, kukatapakaa tope
Zilijaa kila ndiya, isibakiye nyeupe
Ukawa mwingi udhiya, pa kupita zisitupe
Pa kupita zisitupe, kwa ndiya kukosekana
6
Japo hivyo zilikuwa, ndiya hazipitiki
Bali mimi haamuwa, kwenenda japo kwa dhiki
Kumbe vile nitakuwa, ni mfano wa samaki
Ni mfano wa samaki, kuiendeya ndowana

7
Zikanibwaga telezi, sikujuwa kuzendeya
Ningekwenda kwa henezi, yasingemfika haya
Lakini tena siwezi, mwendo huo kutumiya
Sitawata kutembeya, ila tabadili mwendo

– 3 Agosti 1970

Slipperiness

The rain that fell amidst frightening thunder and lightning
In endless quantity from dawn to dusk
Offered no benefit to those tilling the land
Those tilling the land suffered great loss

Seedlings they had planted were uprooted in the deluge
All their hard work came to naught
They harvested none of the fruit they anticipated
The fruit they anticipated remained beyond their reach

Those who feared the rain, lest it drench their bodies
Ran hastily for cover
While others wouldn't rest 'til their homes they reached
'Til their homes they reached and closed the doors shut

Friends, jokes aside, what I am saying truly happened
It carved a deep chasm, this tremendous storm
And the strong currents overflowed in the streets
Overflowed in the streets, even after the rain had ceased

When the rain had stopped it was muddy all over
Mud filled every road, not leaving a single path clean
So inconvenient it was, that we could not discern the way
We could not discern the way, due to impassable roads

Though that is how it was, with roads that were impassable
Still I decided to proceed, despite the hardships
Little did I know, I would be like a fish
I would be like a fish, taking itself onto the hook

I fell on the slippery ground. I did not know how to navigate it
Had I been more cautious, I might have avoided what befell me
But I will never again walk in that fashion
I will not stop walking, though I will change my approach

 — 3 August 1970, *Kamiti Maximum Security Prison, Nairobi, Kenya*

Kibaruwa

Kwenye shamba hilo kubwa asilani hakunyi mvuwa
Ni kwa mitilizi ya jasho langu ndiyo hunweshezewa
Kwenye shamba hilo kubwa sasa imeshaiva kahawa
Na bunize ni matone ya damu yangu niliyotowa
                    Ndipo mte ukatipuza

Buni hiyo itakaangwa buni hiyo itapondwapondwa
Buni hiyo itasagwa na buni hiyo itafyondwafyondwa
Bali itabaki nyeusi kama ngozi yangu Kibaruwa

Waulize ndege kwa nyimbo nyanana watutumbuizao
Iulize na mito kwa furaha maji itiririkao
Uulize na upepo mkali kwa ghadhabu uvumao -
Viulize: Ni nani araukaye na mapema kuzitema mbuga na
   kuzilaza?
Viulize: Ni nani akweaye minazi tangu kuchapo hadi lingiapo giza?
Viulize: Ni nani abebeshwaye mizigo hadi maungo yakageuka shaza?
Halafuye hana faida moja apatayo wala malipo yanayotosheleza -
Isipokuwa kusundugwa na kutupiwa matambara na vyakula
vilivyooza?
Viulize: Ni nani huyo ni nani!

Viulize: Ni nani ayalimaye mashamba na kuyapalilia?
Na mimea kochokocho ikajaa kwa uzito ikajinamia?
Hatimaye nani atajirikaye mali yakammiminikia
Akaota na kitambi kama mja mzito wa miezi tisa
Na akaongeza magari na wanawake kutoka na kuingia?
Viulize: Ni nani huyo ni nani!

Na hao ndege kwa nyimbo nyanana watutumbuizao
Nayo hiyo mito kwa furaha maji itiririkao
Na huo upepo mkali wenye ghadhabu uvumao
Vyote hivyo vitatu vitakujibu kwa umoja wao:
"Ni Kibaruwa Manamba ndiye mtendaji hayo!"

    —*1980s, London*

Casual Laborer

It never rains on that vast field
With streams of my sweat it is watered
And in that vast field coffee trees are ready for harvesting
And the coffee beans are drops of my blood that I have shed
Enabling seedlings to sprout

Those coffee beans will be roasted, those coffee beans will be
 pounded
Those coffee beans will be sucked, those coffee beans will be
 ground
But they will remain black as the color of my skin, the laborer

Ask the birds that serenade us with sweet songs
Ask the rivers that happily flow with water
Ask the strong wind that blows with fury
Ask them: who is the one who wakes early and clears the bush?
Ask them: who is it that climbs the coconut trees from daybreak to
 dusk?
Ask them: who is made to carry loads 'til his back is rough like
 coral?
And then receives no benefit, is not paid a fair wage
Only insulted and tossed tattered clothes and rotten food
Ask them: who is that?

Ask them: who is it that cultivates and weeds the fields?
The plants fruiting so abundantly that they bend with the weight?
Finally, who gets rich with wealth pouring down upon him?
Developing a potbelly like a nine-month pregnancy?
Rotating through a growing number of cars and women?
Ask them: who is that?

And those birds that serenade us with sweet songs
And those rivers that happily flow with water

And that strong wind that blows with fury
All those three will answer you in unison:
"It's the indentured laborer who did all that!"

   — *1980s, London*

The following poem **Ungapomoka** *was written by AA while on a three-month study tour in Mainz, in August 1978, while still on the faculty at UDSM[1]. He received a letter from E. Kezilahabi telling him the news that President Jomo Kenyatta had just died. He wrote this poem in response.*

Ungapomoka

Na mti uangukapo, ungapomoka, pomoko kuu
Taharuki lingawapo, na shabuka, mbasi kwa nduu
Hakwambwi kwa majitapo, kufurahika, ni ubuzyuu
Kwani miziye i papo, itatipuka, yenende juu
Na yaliyopo yawepo, pasi kwondoka, na mti huu!

— 1978, *Mainz*

Although It Has Fallen

Though the tree has fallen with a resounding thud
Though anxiety and worry beset friends and family
One should not speak of it with certitude; rejoicing is foolhardy
Because its roots are still intact, producing new shoots
And what is there will remain, not disappearing with the falling of the tree!

–April 2013, *Berlin*

---

[1] University of Dar es Salaam.

Reem Bassiouney

Letter to Mr. "F" رسالة الى السيد "ف" |
French Fries بطاطس مقلية, |
Until Seven o'Clock حتى الساعة السابعة,

Translated by Xiaoxi Zhang

رسالة الى السيد "ف"

الى السيد الاستاذ "ف"
تحية طيبة وبعد،
لقد اذللتني.. حطمت حياتي
كنت اظن يوما انني امرأة سعيدة.. هادئة ومتعقلة.. لم أكن يوما أنني هكذا..
كيف بدأت القصة؟ أتتذكر ؟

بدأت يوم أتيت من عملي كعادتي وبدأت في اعداد العذاء.. دون أن أفكر للحظة من أكون وأين أكون فأنا هكذا دائما أعمل في ميكانيكية، أنا والموقد لا نختلف كثيرا.. كلانا يحترق في صمت.. وكلانا بارد من الخارج... ما ان بدأت في اعداد الغذاء حتى وقعت عيني على شيء غريب.. وراء دولاب المطبخ.. بلعت ريقي في فزع.. بقايا طعام.. شخصا أكله ثم القى بالبقايا.. بل خبئها في هذا المكان.. رجل.. ربما .. حرامي في بيتي.. أكل بطريقة هادئة.. شامخة. أكل اللحم الابيض للدجاجة فقط.. ترك الأرز وأكل اللحم. حاولت أن أتجاهل هذه الحادثة.. واستمرت حياتي يومين.. ثم تكررت الحادثة من جديد.. من يفعل هذا؟ وماذا يقصد.. زوجي.. الخادمة.. أولادي.. لا أدري.. لا أدري.. ولكن ليت الطعام كان المشكلة الوحيدة بل بدأت أسمع أصواتا غريبة في البيت.. هناك شخص ما يسكن بيتنا. في ميكانيكية. اقتنعت تماما أن البيت مسكون! هذه أعمال جن يسكن معنا و يسخر مني.. إلى من ألجأ؟ وجدت نفسي في ميكانيكية أيضا ألجأ لأخي.. سيتشفى في، أعرف ذلك، فلم أكن يوما أحبه و لكنني حكيت له كل شيء، تأثر وتنهد وذهب في وجوم.. عاد في اليوم التالي وهمس في ألم "نعم.. مسكون.. إمرأة تريد زوجك.. هي من أمرت هذا الجن بأن يفعل هذا.. وسوف يفعل الكثير .... ألا تلاحظين أن أولادكم لا يطيق بعضهم.. البعض.. و زوجك .."

قاطعته في ضيق: إذا كانت تريد زوجي فلتأخذه. إنه رجل لا يطاق على كل حال.. ولكن لماذا تعذبني.. لماذا ؟ لقد تغير كل شيء في البيت كما قلت.. أصبح كل منّا يكره الآخر.. كل هذا من أجل زوجي؟

بدأت مرحلة جديدة من حياتي.. كل يوم أنهي عملي مبكرا.. ثم ألهث وراء الدجالين فيقولون كلهم نفس الشيء.. حاولت وحاولت.. وبالتدريج بدأت حركة الجن تقل بعض الشيء.. وتنفست الصعداء من جديد في خوف من كل شيء حولي.. ثم عاد.. عاد أكثر ضراوة وأشد قسوة.. عاد الجن و بدأت أرجوه.. بالساعات وأبكي.. تارة أقذفه بالشتائم وتارة أرجوه.. لن أتركه يقتلني.. شعرت أن كل من حولي يتآمرون علي... كلهم.. الخادمة.. أطفالي.. وهو.... زوجي هذا.. وكل يوم.. أجد شيئا ما مختلفا في بيتي.. كل يوم أنتظر قدوم الجن وخطواته!

بدأ من حولي يظن أنني مجنونة...ولكنني أمسكت بيد زوجي.. جعلته يرى بعينيه بقايا طعام الجن.. طعام لم أطبخه.. هو أتى به من أسفل الأرض. فهو جن أرضي.. فتح زوجي فمه في ذهول فصرخت في وجهه: لماذا تريدك؟ ألا تعرف حقيقتك؟ ألا تعرف أنني أحمل العبء كله؟ وانت لا تفعل شيئا سوى تحطيم أحلامي.. إنني أكرهك.. لم أحبك يوما!

نظر لي في ذهول.. لم يكن جميلا و لم يكن قبيحا.. كان رجلا عاديا لا يوجد به أي شيء مميز لذا تزوجته ولذا لم أعد أريده.. لم أعد أريد رجلا عاديا.

وما هي أحلامي التي حطمها؟ وهل كان عندي أحلام؟ لم أعد أنام..أسمع صوته في كل لحظة..هذا الجن..السيد "ف"، هكذا أطلقت عليه..لم يعد شيئا ينفع.. علي أن أترك زوجي و أترك الشقة..وأين سأذهب أنا وأولادي؟

تركت عملي..أصبح شغلي الشاغل هو السيد "ف".. لا بد أن يجيبني..لماذا يقسو علي هكذا؟ ألا يكفي أنني لم أعد أريد شيئا..لا بد أن أراه!

و جاء اليوم الذي كنت أتوق إليه.رأيته.
وأنا جالسة أحملق في الحائط في يأس..
شعرت بحمل على أرجلي..بأرجل صغيرة تلذعني..تقتلني.

"فأر!فأر!أنقذوني!"

كان فأرا إذن..فأرا..حطم شيئا بداخلي.. فأرا جعلني أتصرف بهستيرية..لم أكن لأستريح حتى أراه أمامي جثة هامدة! سأنتقم منه هذا القاسي..سأفعل
وجاء أخي بالسم.
آسفة يا سيد "ف" ولكنك قاس!
وشكرا!
همس السيد "ف" في لحظاته الأخيرة "سيدتي أنا بريء" ومات.

LETTER TO MR. "F"

To the esteemed Mr. "F,"
    Greetings,
    You humiliated me. You destroyed my life.
    I once thought every day I was a happy woman . . . quiet and prudent. I never thought I was like this.
    How does the story begin? Do you remember?
    It started one day when I came back from work and was cooking . . . without thinking for a moment who I was and where I came from. I always work like this, mechanically. I am not very different from an incinerator. We both burn silently and are cold on the outside. I was starting to prepare the meal when something strange happened. Behind the kitchen cupboard . . . I swallowed my saliva in panic . . . food! Someone had eaten food and hidden the rest here. A man . . . probably. A thief in my house. He had eaten quietly, loftily. He had eaten only the white chicken meat. . . . He had left the rice and eaten the meat. I tried to ignore it. . . . My life went on for two

more days. Then I remembered it again. Who did this? What does this mean . . . my husband . . . the maid . . . my children . . . I don't know . . . I don't know. I wished the food were the only problem but I began to hear strange noises. There was someone living in our house. My first reaction was to be convinced the house was haunted! This was the work of a genie who had taken up residence to mock me. To whom should I turn? I resorted to my brother. He would not be of any help, I knew, since I had never loved him, but I told him everything anyway. He was troubled, sighed, and left in silence. He came back the next day and whispered with difficulty: Yes . . . it is haunted . . . a woman desires your husband . . . she called upon genie . . . he is doing all this. Didn't you notice your children cannot stand each other . . . and your husband . . .

I cut him off, if she wants my husband, let her have him. He is unbearable after all . . . But why does she torture me . . . Why? Everything in the house has changed, everything between us is hatred . . . All this because of my husband?

A new stage of my life began. Every day I finish work early. Then I breathed behind the antichrist since they all say the same thing . . . I tried and tried . . . Gradually the genie's activity tapered off. I breathed a sigh of relief in fear of everything around me. Then he came back, fiercer and more severely. The genie came back and I started to beg him . . . for hours and hours and to cry. . . . Sometimes I cursed him and sometimes I entreated him . . . I will not let him kill me . . . I felt that everything was conspiring against me . . . all of them . . . the maid . . . my children . . . and him . . . that husband of mine. Every day, I found something different in my house. Every day I waited for the genie and his footsteps!

People started to think I was crazy. But I held my husband's hand. I forced him to see the remains of the genie's food with his own eyes. The food I did not cook. It had come with him from beneath the earth. My husband opened his mouth in astonishment and I screamed at him: Why does she want you? Doesn't she know who you are? Doesn't she know that I bear the burden? That you have done nothing but smash my dreams. I hate you! I never loved you, not even for one day!

He looked at me in astonishment. He wasn't handsome and he

wasn't ugly. He was an average man, nothing special. I married him and no longer wanted him. I no longer wanted an average man.

What were those smashed dreams of mine? Had I ever had a dream? I no longer sleep. I hear his voice every moment . . . this genie . . . Mr. "F" as I call him. Nothing helps. I have to leave my husband and the apartment . . . where can I go with my children?

I quit my work . . . Mr. "F" has become all I can think about. He must answer me. Why is he hardening me like this? Isn't it enough that I no longer want anything? I had to see him!

So the day came when I . . . I saw him. I was sitting beside the wall in despair . . . I felt a weight on my legs . . . I felt a little leg tickling me . . . killing me . . .

"Mouse! Mouse! Save me!"

It was a mouse so . . . a mouse. He destroyed something within me . . . the mouse made me act hysterically . . . I couldn't rest until I saw his corpse before me! Lifeless! I will avenge this hardness. I will do it. My brother came with poison. Sorry Mr. "F" but you are cruel!

And thank you!

In his last moments Mr. "F" whispered, "My Miss, I am innocent," and he died.

بطاطس مقلية

لا شيء يثير ضيقي كالنساء، وخاصة زوجتي، يتصبب منها الكره لي..أعرف ذلك..رأيته في عينيها منذ ثلاثين عاما ولم أزل أراه في عينيها وسوف أراه في عينيها. تكرهني هذه المرأة ثم ماذا؟

تنوي أن تقضي علي..ستقتلني ستفعل عاجلا أو أجلا ستفعل وقد اختارت الوقت المناسب. هرم مثلي في السادسة والستين لن يقو على المقاومة.

أين أيام شبابي عندما كنت أصرخ في وجهها فتدمع عينيها ويتصبب منها العرق وتنكمش فتذكرني بطبق "الكرشة" الممتلىء بالصلصة. ولا أبالي، لم أكن أبالي.

لا تحاول أن تهديء إمرأة تبكي، سوف تظن أنك رجل ضعيف. ستقتلني يوما هذه المرأة..أرى هذا في عينيها. تزوجتها لماذا؟ لأن أنفها رقيق..ولماذا يتزوج الرجل من المرأة؟ دائما من أجل أنفها والآن بعد أن التهم الروماتيزم ظهري....وذراعي وأرجلي أصبحت كالأسد الجريح والصياد يستمتع بالقاء السهم على أسد جريح. والزوجة تريد أن تستمتع بضعفي.. لن أترك لها الفرصة قلت لها مرارا إن صوت الملعقة يثير أعصابي وهاهي تقلب الشاي في لامبالاة وكأنها لا تقصد إثارة أعصابي القاسية! في شيخوختي تريد الانتقام!

"إنني اكرهك" قالتها لي كثيرا وكان جزاؤها في الماضي صفعة قوية كصفعات أفلام زمان. كانت بعدها تدمع في صمت، القاسية تريد النيل مني الآن. ولم تزل تقلب الشاي بالملعقة يف لامبالاه. صوت الملعقة يصم أذني

"كفي عن هذا!!"

لم تسمعني

"يا إمرأة كفي عن هذا"

ابتسمت في هدوء وأخذت تقلب الشاي ثم همست: إنني أقلب كوب الشاي ألم تطلب مني شايا؟

وضعت به سما..سأبلغ البوليس..سأفعل..اين إولادي؟ لماذا تركوها تنال مني؟ ارتجفت يدي دائما ترتجف هذه الأيام. ليت يدي لا ترتجف أمامها.

حملقت في يدي المرتجفة. تسخر مني..تتشفى في ضعفي..ستدفع الثمن..سأقتلها أنا أو لا! نعم..ولكن كيف؟
حرقا ربما ولم لا؟

سوف أطلب منها شيئا، أي شيء ثم تشعل نار الموقد ثم أتصرف أنا..

قلت في صرامة: أريد بطاطس مقلية الآن.

حملقت في دهشة ثم اتجهت الى المطبخ، اشعلت النار، وضعت الطاسة ثم الزيت.. صوت الزيت يؤلمني كصوت زوجتي تماما.. ها هي الساعة قد حانت، اتكأت على العصا.. اتجهت إلى المطبخ.. نظرت إلى السكين التي في يدها تقطع بها البطاطس ثم تلقي بها في الزيت فيتلوى.. يحترق.. اغمضت عيني.. رائحة البطاطس جميلة.

ليس علي أن أقتلها الآن.. ربما بعد أن آكل البطاطس ثم ألا يكفي أنني شفيت غليلي ورأيت البطاطس تتلوى ألما؟ سآكل البطاطس أو لا و ربما أجعلها تأكل معي فأنا أكره أن آكل بمفرد ولنؤجل القتل.

ابتسمت لها في كبرياء فودت الابتسامة

همست لها: إنك لست شديدة القسوة على كل حال.. كل النساء قاسيات، لن ألومك على شيء ليس بيدك.. متى سنأكل البطاطس؟

FRENCH FRIES

Nothing is as troubling as women, and my wife especially, nothing but hatred comes from her towards me ... I know that. I saw the hatred in her eyes from thirty years ago, I still see it in her eyes, and I will still see it in the future. This woman hates me, then what?

She wants to eliminate me ... She will kill me sooner or later, she will, and she has chosen the right time. An old man like me at the age of sixty-six will not have the strength to resist.

Where are the days of my youth when I yelled in her face and her eyes would blink, and she would sweat and shrink and then remind me of my dish. The "kursha" full of sauce. I didn't care, I never really cared.

Do not try to calm a crying woman, for she will take you to be a weak man. This woman she will kill me one day ... I see this in her eyes. Why did I marry her? Because her nose is petite. And why should a man marry a woman? Always because of her nose. After rheumatism devoured my back ... and my arm and my legs, I became a wounded lion, and the hunter enjoys throwing arrows at a wounded lion, and this wife of mine wants to take advantage of my distress. I will not leave this chance to her. I told her repeatedly that the sound of the spoon gets on my nerves and here she stirs the tea indifferently, as if she doesn't care about my stirring nerves. Cruel! She wants to avenge when I am senile!

"I hate you!" She often said this to me. And her recompense in the past used to be a strong blow in the face, like the blows in the old-time movies. After that she would weep in silence, so cruel that she wants to get rid of me now. And the way she stirs the tea with her spoon is not indifferent. The sound of the spoon deafens my ears.

"Enough of this!"

She didn't hear me.

"Woman, this is enough!"

She smiled quietly, stirred the tea and then whispered: "I am stirring a cup of tea, didn't you ask me for tea?"

She put poison in it . . . I will call the police . . . I will. Where are my children? Why they let her get back at me? My hands trembled as they often do these days. Would my hands not tremble in front of her!

I clasped my trembling hands. She makes fun of me . . . She heals in my weakness . . . She will pay the price. Will I kill her or not! Yes . . . but how?

Burning maybe, and why not?

I will ask for something from her, anything, and then she would turn on the fire at the stove, then I take my action . . .

Sternly, I said: "I want French fries, now!"

She was astonished and then turned to the kitchen. She turned on the fire, put the pan on it and then the oil . . . the sound of the oil hurts me just like the sound of my wife. The hour has come, I leaned on the stick . . . I turned to the kitchen . . . I saw the knife in her hands which she used to cut the potatoes and then she took them to the oil, and they twisted, burned . . . I closed my eyes . . . The fries smell wonderful.

I should not kill her now . . . maybe after I eat the fries . . . isn't it enough that I get back at her. I looked at the fries squirming out of pain. I will eat the French fries first, maybe I will let her eat with me, since I hate eating by myself. So let's postpone the killing.

I smiled at her proudly and she smiled back.

I whispered to her: "You are not very cruel anyhow . . . all women are cruel. I am not going to blame you for things beyond your control . . . When will we eat the fries?"

<u>حتى الساعة السابعة</u>

يقولون إنه يريدني في شيء هام. رجل غريب حقا. إنني بالكاد أعرفه. رأيته مرة أو مرتين وأنا أعطي ابن مدير منزله درسا خصوصيا، يقولون إن مصيبة قد حلت على رأسه..فقد كل أمواله، كان يقوم بأعمال غير مشروعة..سينتهي به الأمر في السجن..بل هو شيوعي، بل اقطاعي، المال ينسكب من بدلته الأنيقة..ارستقراطي، والده كان وزيرا للداخلية سابق، بل صاحب أراض..على كل، صوته هو ما يعجبني فيه. لا يصرخ أبدا. صوته كحروف الآلة الكاتبة تأتي كلها متساوية . ترى لماذا يريدني؟ أخرجت المرأة حملقت في شعري المفروق من الوسط. حملقت في عيوني الذابلة، بدا السن عليهما. "الحياة خدعتك وشطبت ثلاثين عاما من عمرك" لم يحاول أحد أن يغازلني منذ زمن. المشكلة أنني لست كبقية البنات..حمقاء، لا أعرف الطرق الملتوية للنساء. ترى لماذا يريدني هذا الرجل؟

الساعة الآن الخامسة.

جلست في انتظار الرجل..دخل..ابتسم لي في فتور جلس أمامي، ثم ساد الصمت. عيناه غريبة حقا فهي كسن القلم الرصاص المبري بعناية. همس للخادمة: أريد طبق فستق ثم العشاء.

الرجل مجنون حقا..عشاء ماذا؟ هل يظن أنني واحدة من هؤلاء؟ تكلمت..لم يجب. أخذ ينظر حوله في حيرة طفل أخرجوه من عالمه البريء إلى عالم لا يعرفه ولا يفهمه ثم قال في صرامة: لن تذهبي اليوم.

بلعت ريقي في ذهول وقلت: ماذا؟

- لأن تذهبي اليوم..قلت لي ما اسمك؟ اعذريني أنني أنسى بسرعة هذه مشكلتي، فهناك أشياء تشغل بالي هذه الأيام، أردتك لأعقد معك صفقة. (وأنا من ظننت أن الحظ قد ابتسم لي أخيرا!)

ثم استرسل: ما رأيك في الحياة؟

فتحت فمي فقال مسرعا: هل أكلت من قبل طبق فلافل؟ ما ألذها.

- استاذ..

قاطعني: سأجعلك تتذوقين اليوم صلصلة الغستق..هل جربتيها من قبل؟ إنني أعشق الفستق لذا تجدينني دائما آكله على العشاء..رز بالفستق، سلطة بالفستق، صلصلة بالفستق، لحم بالفستق، وفستق! قلت لي ما اسمك؟ قمت في هدوء لأفتح الباب و أخرج فالرجل يبدو مجنونا لكنه امسك بيدي في برائته الغريبة و.. همس في رقة لم أكن أعرفها: أرجوك لا تذهبي أنني أحتاجك.

بلعت ريقي..خرجت مني رجفة ثم ابتسمت لنفسي.....يحبني بالطبع!

التفت حوله من جديد في حيرة، نادى على الخادمة وسأل: هل جاء المأذون أم لم يأت بعد؟

قالت في خوف: جاء يا سيدي.

وجدت اطرافي ترتجف وهويت الى المقعد في ذهول..أكان يحبني منذ زمن ولم أكن أدري؟

قال وهو يجلس أمامي في حماس غريب وهو يلوح بيده في عصبية كطفل يريد شيئا: سنتزوج الآن..هل جربتي عصير الفستق..إنه جميل.
قلت في تلقائية: أنا لا أوافق!
- لماذا؟ ألا تحبينني؟ لا تقولي إنك لا تحبينني..لقد رأيت الحب في عينيك..أنا لا أنسى شيئا رأيته!
فتحت فمي ثم اغلقته من جديد. أغمضت عيني و دمعة مريرة تتساقط منهما، حلم غويب هذا!!
اقترب مني وهو يهمس: إنني أعرف كل شيء عنك....أحب كل شيء فيك.
تزوجته ولا أدري كيف أكلت الفستق وأنا زوجته ثم طلبت من الخادمة أن تعد لنا طبق فلافل. حملق في براءة فجلست بجانبه وبدأت أضع الأكل في فمه وكأنه طفل صغير، طاقات حنان لم أكن أعرفها، لم أكن يوما حنونة و لكنه رجل غويب!
ابتسم لي ..أشعرني بشعور غريب، أنني "انا" أدخله عالم لا يعرفه..أن كل شيء يفعله معي، حتى مذاق الفلافل غريب وجديد.
ثم همس في رقة وهو يمسك يدي: علي أن أخبرك بشيء هام..علينا أن نصحو غدا في السابعة صباحا!
قلت في دهشة وكأنه أيقظني من حلم جميل: لماذا؟ أعني..نسيت....علي..علي أن أذهب الآن..والدتي..
قاطعني في ضيق: لا تذهبي الآن ..إنني أحتاجك.
قام في هدوء..فتح درج مكتبه وأخرج علبتين....أعطاني واحدة ثم فتحها فوجدت فيها خاتما بديعا من الماس الخالص، ارتجفت يدي وأنا أنظر له، فقال هو مسرعا: أتعرفين كم ثمنه؟ ثلثمائة ألف جنيه.. للأسف لن أستطيع أن أشتريه لك..لقد اقتزضته اليوم..وسوف أعيده غدا في السابعة!
نظرت له في نفس الدهشة ثم قلت في تردد: لا أفهم.
- يمكنك ان ترتديه حتى السابعة..ما رأيك يا..قلت لي ما اسمك؟ أنا آسف أنه مرض النسيان هذا..هل من الأفضل أن ترتدي خاتما ماسيا جميلا كهذا لساعات فقط، أم من الأفضل أن تحي حياتك طوال حياتك ما تعرفين ما هو الماس؟
قلت مسرعة: بالطبع من الأفضل أن أرتديه ساعات!
- حياتنا هكذا يا حبيبتي حزمة من الساعات المتناثرة نقترضها ثم نعيدها وأنا قررت أن أعيدها في السابعة وأنت معي.
ابتسمت في هدوء: نعيد الخاتم نعيد حياتنا.
فتح العلبة الأخرى، بها زجاجة صغيرة، ابتسم وهو يهمس: سم..سوف أقتل نفسي في السابعة فالساعات القادمة لي في هذا العالم ستصبح بدون الخاتم لذا علي أن انهيها. حتى الفستق نفذت كميته، لم يعد يبقى سوى ساعات وانت معي.
شهقت في فزع: معك أين؟

- لقد اخترتك أنت.
- لتقتلني؟ إنك.. إنك متعب ويائس ، الانتحار لن يفيد.. في الصباح..
- في الصباح سوف استمتع بأعظم انتصاراتي بقدرتي على ان أسيطر على إنسان، في الصباح ستشربين السم معي بإرادتك، ويكفيني ما حققته من انتصارات حتى الآن.

أحمق ومجنون.. في الصباح سأبلغ البوليس ليمنعه وحتى لو لم يمنعه فيكفي أنني سأبقى حية.. ربما علي أن أرحل الآن، ولم لا أنتظر حتى الصباح؟

كل ما يفعله لن يفلح معي، كلماته غويبة، براءته المصحوبة بحماس شاب وعصبية هرم وضعف طفل. كل هذا لن يفلح معي. عندما أعود.. سوف.. سوف أبدا حياة جديدة، فحياتي القديمة كانت شديدة الملل. ربما اتزوج غيره.. كان حلمي أن اتزوج و قد تحقق ولن أجد رجلا مثله.. لبس علي أن اتزوج إذن. ألحبه؟ هل أبلغ البوليس الآن؟ فلأنتظر ساعتين حتى السابعة. فلأبقى معه حتى السابعة فربما لا أراه بعد الآن. كلماته غويبة .أكاد أفقد صوابي.. شيطان هو أم ماذا؟ ماذا أتى بي إلى هنا؟ فلأنتظر حتى السابعة .

حملقت في عينيه فابتسم في ثقة وهمس: تخافين؟
قلت في يأس: فات أوان الخوف فقد شربت السم.
- لم يزل أمامك نصف ساعة.
- قلت في فتور: لقد وعدتني أنني لن اتألم.
- يمكنك أن تستغيثي.
ابتسمت في جفاء وهمست في مرارة: لماذا فعلت بي هذا؟
- أتصدقينني لو قلت إني أحبك؟
- لا لن أصدقك.
- أتصدقينني لو قلت لك إنني كذبت عليك.. والدي كان غفيرا والفلافل كانت أكلتنا المفضلة.. لم أكن ارستقراطيا، لو كنت قابلتك منذ عشر سنوات كنت ستصبحين بالنسبة لي أميرة.

قلت وقد بدأت أفقد السيطرة على عقلي: لن أصدق هذا أيضا.

قام.. قبل جبهتي في احترام شديد ثم جلس وهمس: إنك امرأة شجاعة.. قلت لي ما اسمك؟

UNTIL SEVEN O'CLOCK

They say that he wants me for something important. Really a strange man. I barely even know him. I saw him once or twice as I gave private lessons to the son of his house manager. They say that a disaster has come upon him . . . since all his fortunes were acquired through illegal acts. He will end up in prison . . . whether he is a communist or a feudal lord, wealth shows through his stylish suit . . . aristocratic, his father was Minister of Interior in the past, but landowner . . . anyway, it is his voice what I like about him. He never shouts. His voice sounds like the letters of the typewriter, all of them come out equal. See why he wants me? I took out the mirror, stared at my hair parted in the middle . . . I stared at my withered eyes, which started to show the trace of age. "Life deceived you and wrote thirty years off your age" no one tried to flirt with me for a long while. The problem is that I am not like the other girls . . . idiot, I don't know the twisted manners for women. I wonder why this man wants me.

Now five o'clock.

I sat waiting for the man . . . he came in . . . smiled at me chillingly, sat in front of me, then silence prevailed. His eyes were really strange as they were like carefully sharpened pencil head. He whispered to the maid: I want a pistachio dish then dinner.

The man is really crazy . . . Dinner? What? Does he think that I am one of them? So I talked, he did not answer. He looked around in the confusion of a child getting out from his innocent world to a world he does not know nor understand, then he said in sternness: You will not go today.

I swallowed my saliva in astonishment and said: "What?"

"Because if you go today . . . Miss . . . Did you tell me what is your name? Excuse me as I forget quickly, this problem of mine, there are many things occupying me these days, I wanted you to make a deal with you."

Then he continued: "What is your opinion about life?" (And I thought that luck finally smiled at me!)

I opened my mouth and he said quickly: "Have you had falafel dish before? How tasty . . ."

"Mr. . . ."

He cut me off: "I will make you taste the pistachio sauce today . . . Have you tried it before? I adore pistachios so much that's why you always find me eating it at dinner . . . rice with pistachios, salad with pistachios, sauce with pistachios, meat with pistachios, and pistachios! Did you tell me what is your name?"

I stood up silently to open the door and leave as the man seems crazy, but he held my hand with strange innocence and murmured in a delicate manner that I don't understand: "Please do not go, I need you!"

I swallowed my saliva . . . a shiver came out of me then I smiled at myself . . . he loves me of course.

He turned around once more in confusion, he called the maid and asked: "Has the marriage authorizing officer arrived or not?"

She said in fear: "He came my sir."

I found my limbs trembling and fell to my seat in astonishment . . . Could it be that he loved me for a long time and I just didn't know?

Sitting in front of me in a flare of enthusiasm and waving his hands nervously like a child wanting something, he said: "We are going to get married now . . . Have you tried pistachio juice? It is nice!"

I said instinctively: "I don't agree."

"Why? Don't you love me? Don't tell me that you don't love me . . . I already saw love in your eyes . . . I don't forget anything that I saw . . ."

I opened my mouth and then closed it again. I closed my eyes, from where a bitter drop of tear came out, what a strange dream that is.

He approached me while whispering: "I know everything about you . . . I love everything in you."

I married him and I don't know how I ate the pistachios and I am his wife, then I asked the maid to prepare a falafel dish for us. He stared innocently as I sat next to him and started to put food into his mouth, as if he was a little child. I did not know the power of affection, I was never affectionate even for a day but he is a strange man.

He smiled at me . . . he made me feel strange, that "I" am introducing him to a world he doesn't know . . . that everything he does with me, even the taste of falafel is strange and new.

Then he gently whispered, holding my hands: "I have to tell you something important . . . we have to wake up tomorrow at seven in the morning!"

I said in astonishment as if he woke me up from a sweet dream: "Why? I mean . . . I forgot . . . I . . . I have to go now . . . my mother . . ."

He cut me off, annoyed: "Don't go now . . . I need you."

He got up quietly . . . opened the drawer of his desk and took out two boxes . . . he gave me one, then opened it, and I found an exquisite diamond ring, my hand shivered and I looked at him, and he said quickly: "You know how much it costs? Three hundred thousand Egyptian pounds . . . Unfortunately I won't be able to buy it for you . . . I borrowed it today . . . and I will return it tomorrow at seven!"

I looked at him in the same astonishment then I said, hesitantly: "I don't understand."

"You can wear it until seven . . . What do you think Miss . . . Did you tell me what is your name? I am sorry about this forgetfulness . . . Is it better to wear a beautiful diamond ring like this for only a few hours, or is it better to live all your life not knowing what a diamond is?"

I said quickly: "Of course it is better to wear it for a few hours!"

"Our life is like this my dear, a bundle of scattered hours, we borrow it then we return it, and I decided to return it at seven o'clock and you are with me."

I smiled quietly: "We give back the ring."

"We give back our life."

He opened the second box, in which there is a small bottle, he smiled and whispered: "Poison . . . I will kill myself at seven, for the upcoming few hours for me in this world will be without the ring so I have to finish it. Even the pistachios ran out. There are only few hours left and you are with me."

I gasped in panic: "With you, where to?"

"I have chosen you."

"For you to kill me? You are . . . You are tired and desperate, suicide will not help . . . in the morning . . ."

"In the morning I will enjoy the greatest of my victories, with my ability to control a human being. In the morning you will drink the poison with me at your own will, it's enough of what I have achieved until now."

A foolish and crazy person . . . In the morning I will call the police to stop him, and if they wouldn't stop him from doing this, then it would be enough for me to stay alive . . . Maybe I have to leave now, or why don't I wait until the morning?

All what he's doing will not work with me. His words are strange. His innocence is accompanied by the enthusiasm of a young man, the nerves of an old man, and the weakness of a child. All this will not work with me. When I return . . . I will . . . I will start a new life, for my old life was too tedious. Maybe I marry someone else . . . Marriage was my dream and it came true and there will be no one like him . . . I do not have to marry then. Do I love him? Do I call the police now? I will wait for two hours until seven o'clock. I will stay with him until seven o'clock as I might not see him anymore. His words are strange. I am about to lose my mind . . . Is he a devil or what? What brought me here? We'll wait until seven.

I stared in his eyes and he smiled confidently and whispered: "Are you afraid?"

I said in despair: "The time for fear is over because I drank the poison."

"You have less than half an hour."

I said in a state of torpor: "You promised me that I will not be in pain."

"You can ask for help."

I smiled indifferently and whispered bitterly: "Why did you do this to me?"

"Do you believe me if I told you I love you?"

"No I won't trust you."

"Do you believe me if I tell you I lied to you . . . My father was a watch guard and falafel was our favorite dish . . . I was not an aristocrat. If I met you ten years ago you would be a princess for me."

Starting to lose control of my mind, I said: "I won't believe this either."

He got up . . . and kissed my forehead in keen respect, then sat and whispered: "You are a brave woman . . . Did you tell me what is your name?"

Untitled 2018 | Njabulo Dzonzi

Nyambura Mpesha
M-Diag | Nani?, Who?

Translated by the author

M-DIAG[1]

Uanzaye mwaka mosi sikiliza za DIAG
Ipo hapo mbele, puani pa Hatcher

Habari hizi sikiliza
    Si mzaha, si mchezo
        Iko wazi ya buluu, na herufi yake
            M
'Sikanyage 'sichezee, uko mwaka mosi
'Kikanyaga 'taanguka, mitihani utafeli
Utafeli, utashindwa
Miaka yote utashindwa
'Sikanyage M-DIAG

Ni mwiko!

M-DIAG

You starting first year, listen about DIAG
It's there in front of Hatcher's nose

Listen to these news
    It's not a joke, it's not a game
        It's open, in blue, its letter
            M
Don't step on it, don't play with it, in first year
Step on it, you'll fail, you'll fall, exams you'll fail
You'll fail, defeated
    All years defeated
Don't step on M-DIAG
It's taboo!

---

[1] This poem was written in Swahili for my Swahili students. I could not find a better title in Swahili because M-DIAG is presented as a proper noun and I wanted the readers to recognize the place name. Translating the poem into English proved challenging. The verbs –ANGUKA, –FELI, -SHINDWA mean the same thing and in Swahili they are emphatic. The English words FAIL, FALL, and DEFEATED do not seem to convey the same seriousness. The Swahili poem and its English translation have different rhythms. Hatcher Library is personified as having a nose but the image only makes sense in Swahili suggesting the proximity of M-DIAG with reference to Hatcher as similar to the proximity EYE to NOSE on a human body.

Nani?[2]

Walinizunguka wengi wao
Bila kunipa shikamoo
Na mie nikanyamaza
Nione walilowaza
Ya mkongwe wa misimu elfu.

Mwanifungiani jamani
Mwanivuta kwa nini
Tangu lini akahama
Mzee wa misimu elfu, kahama
Mmesikia wapi kahama?

Japo sitembei
Nyumba ninazo mbili
Ya sasa ya lazima
Japo si ya kuazima
Na ya kwanza nisahau.

---

[2]The poem was first written in Swahili when a tree was removed from the University of Michigan's campus. It was written as a riddle for Intermediate Swahili students. With time the tree has been forgotten and often the students are not able to decipher the riddle. The answer to question WHO is THE BUSINESS SCHOOL TREE. This riddle is used when the class is learning Swahili riddles and conundrums.

Who?

Many surrounded me
Without a respectful greeting
I kept silent
To see their plan
Concerning the old one of a thousand seasons.

Why tie me
Why pull me
Since when did one move
An old one of a thousand seasons
Where did you hear of such a move?

Though I don't walk
I have two homes
The current one is forced on me
Though not a borrowed one
And the first I forget.

Mukoma Wa Ngugi

Kidane-Diva "Come See the Other Me," from *We Sing the Tizita to Unbury Our Dead with Song*

"Come See the Other Me!"[1]

By the time I made it back, Kidane was serving Mohamed and the kids hastily scrambled eggs. They had a good laugh at my expense. She went to the kitchen to toast some bread only to hear her curse so loudly that we all went quiet. Mohamed asked what the matter was, and she marched and furiously placed a small loaf of bread with no crust on the table. Then I remembered Mohamed and I high the night before, the munchies demanding something sweet and the only thing we could find was bread. Mohamed had insisted he was going to make me the best peanut butter and jelly sandwich – it involved eating toasted crunchy crust. It was the best P&J sandwich I had ever had but we had not anticipated the fall out. The kids did not mind though, so it balanced out in the end.

It was time to leave for the concert – the set up and rehearsals were going to eat up the rest of the day. The kids were also eager to play football with their father, so after quick casual goodbyes, we were on our way. The same cab driver that dropped us off two days ago was waiting for us at the end of the painful, now that I was invalid with blistered feet, long trek. But I had to make it.

"Shall I stop at the other place?" He asked as soon we got in.

"Yes," she replied.

"What other place?" I asked her.

"You will see," she answered and they both laughed.

The cab driver's name I now learned was Mustafa, a Somali living in Addis and I guess until he had seen you twice, he maintained his cover. Xenophobia against Somali people anytime the war in the Ogaden flared up was a constant fear. We spoke about xenophobia all over the continent, South Africa, Libya, Egypt, it seemed Pan-Africanism was in spirit and not in practice. We talked about Al-Shabab and how the Islamic Court Unions might have done some good were it not for Ethiopia and the United States. And how now Kenya had finally invaded Somalia "officially."

The conversation moved on to the mundane, the cost of bread,

---

[1]Excerpted from *We Sing the Tizita to Unbury Our Dead with Song*, a forthcoming novel by Mukoma Wa Ngugi to be published by Cassava Republic Press. The novel is written in English.

petrol and so on until we were back in Addis where he drove to an expensive looking building a few hundred yards from the African Union headquarters. I thought we were picking up someone but we drove to the back where he punched a few keys into a pad and large gates opened up to a garage. I asked Kidane again where we were going. She simply smiled. Mustafa parked his taxi next to a long Mercedes Benz that looked all the more new next to his Oldsmobile. We entered an elevator where he once again punched a code and we took the long ride up to the top floor to pick up whom I now was sure was a good friend, or Kidane's lover.

When it turned out he had the key to an immaculately furnished penthouse apartment and there was no one in, I started to suspect that they were lovers. They went to respective rooms. The suspense was killing my tabloid senses so I started looking for clues – there were none. I looked at the magazines and newspapers on the glass coffee table. Before I could open the latest Ebony Magazine with barely dressed hips thrust into the camera, Beyoncé on its cover, Kidane, and shortly thereafter Mustafa, returned.

Only it was not Mustafa and Kidane, it was the Diva and her bodyguard. The Diva came over to where I was standing frozen, mouth open, at once understanding what was before me and at the same time as confused as I had ever been. She was dressed in a long white tight evening gown, a light shawl covered with the Ethiopian flag colors, green, yellow and red wrapped around her bare shoulders, her long muscular neck naked. In white sneakers, she was a picture of a quiet sexiness.

Mustafa was dressed in a tuxedo and where before he had seemed thin and effeminate, even in his several sizes bigger shirts and trousers, the Mustafa that stood before me was a guy you did not want to mess with, his chest straining the shirt buttons as he adjusted a gun in his shoulder holster, put on his jacket and checked himself in the mirror to make sure that the gun was concealed. I recognized him – he was the man I had almost run into back at the ABC when I was leaving the Diva's dressing room.

"What is going on? I saw you at the ABC," I said to him.

He shrugged and smiled.

"What's going?" I asked the Diva.

She went over to the stack of magazines and newspapers, took one and threw it at me so that it fell by my feet. And that is when I saw *The National Inquisitor* headline: "The Singer on Top: Drugs, Sex and competition in Nairobi" – the piece in which I had lied in order to bulldoze the moneymen at *The National Inquisitor* to send me to Ethiopia. If the Diva had it, then others surely had seen it.

"You are not the only one with secrets," she said with a laugh when I started trying to explain.

They walked to the door and for a moment I thought they would leave me behind.

"Come," she commanded and I followed them, less a journalist and more like a boy with a crush caught lying. Mustafa flashed me a sympathetic, even friendly smile.

What had I been thinking? And why was she letting me carry on? Whatever the case, I was going to give my readers a good story, regardless of the truth. I mean, had I written only about the Diva of Nairobi, would that have been the truth? Or if I wrote only about Kidane, wife and dutiful mother – would that have been the truth? In a world of multiple covers and faces, only a fool would think the truth was the first face one saw. In journalism school, we used to have drunken debates in the same parties where I played my one Malaika song about objective reporting. Ever the radicals, we would agree there was nothing like objective reporting.

But we had it all wrong because we placed the burden of objectivity on the journalists who in turn bring their biases to the story, to be piled on by the biases of the editor dictated by whatever corporation owned the paper. But we always assumed the subject of the reportage was objectively solid and stable. Well, what I was learning, or rather seeing, confirmed that both the journalist and the subject were in constant motion. And if both of you stopped and talked over a cup of coffee or a beer, that would be a sliver of the truth at that point in time. We had been applying the uncertainty principle to the wrong party; both the journalist and the subject were in constant motion.

Kidane and the Diva, Mustafa the taxi driver and Mustafa the dangerous looking bodyguard in a tuxedo, my many selves and *The National Inquisitor* reporter. All that was beside the point – the question was why Kidane was letting me see her many truths or lies and whether the other musicians would do the same. I was now all the more intrigued to a point of testing my sanity by her.

The Addis Ababa Stadium & Millennium Hall – magnificence on steroids – a country conscious of its image as the poster child of development. In many ways the stadium itself was performing for the TV cameras, the blog writers and tweeters because each story, whether it's about a football game, a political speech or music performance has to begin with its vastness, filled with 60,000 people all here to watch, listen and commune. 60,000 people in one space produce electricity, current charged with anticipation, and in the constant loud indecipherable murmur of talking and singing voices.

She is here to do a benefit concert for soldiers, veterans, families, friends and anyone who cares to show up. It is free, so it's 60,000 people and probably another five thousand standing outside the stadium, not to mention those watching from home. Backstage, the Diva standing there surrounded by tech people, journalists, fans who had won backstage passes, the Diva surrounded by the machinery that produces the music we consume looks so small, in danger of being crushed by all of it. She smiles, signs this, takes a photo, kisses someone on the cheek, shares a joke with an old friend. I look again – she is not in danger of being crushed by it all, she is in control, the skillful surfer who seems to be in danger of being swallowed by a massive wave but triumphs each time. Every now and then she looks at Mustafa, the leash will keep her tied safely to her surfboard if the rising waters were to push her off.

The anticipation builds; the band, all men dressed in army jackets over khaki pants and army boots are playing as if on a loop, repeating the phrase so that each time they return to where the musician should make an entrance, the crowd yells for the Diva. She calls me over and the waters respectfully part to let me through and she whispers, "Come see the other me." She smiles at Mustafa and he walks me over to a small VIP section and then hurries back. I can hear and feel the ocean of 60,000 people behind me. I am no longer a journalist – I am one of them.

I look around and see large screen monitors set up all around the stadium show her making her way to the front of the stage, Mustafa in front of her. The look on her face, triumph mixed with a self-conscious smile that suggests she knows how good she is play on her face. The Diva – Kidane transfigured into the Diva – walks onto the stage. The united horn section goes into high gear, the drums, bass and keyboards follow and a storm of dancing song brews. She walks up and down the stage, she owns it – she stops every now and then, says something and playfully wags a finger at the crowd – I have no idea what the words mean, but I know enough now not to worry about what words mean but what her voice says – she is telling the men to be careful of her, or of others like her, or telling the women to be wary of men like the ones she is pointing at.

Call and response with the band, the horn section coming in slightly before she talks to the men, more like sings to them with the band all quiet and then as her voice gets angrier yet playful the band comes in. The drums set the tone – a few angry rat-a-tats as the horn section, the keyboards and the Diva remain silent – and then her, just her, her voice speaking to the 60,000 people comes in, magnified by the image of the beautiful lone woman on stage and we all go wild, the band comes in – and we are hungry for more.

She paces up and down stage, her voice whipping up the band into a frenzy – and then she does a simple gesture that almost causes a riot – the band comes to a stop, there is only silence. She runs to the center of the stage and takes off her suit jacket – and then runs her fingers over the buttons of her white shirt, pretending to undo each one of them. The roar of a turned-on crowd – the band intervenes but not before letting one of the trumpet players talk to her – his trumpet approving, asking for more. It is in a word the sexiest, most erotic performance I have ever witnessed and I feel things in me stirring, made all the more intense by a turned-on, massive crowd. And then she moves on to a few more disco-music like tunes – we dance and dance, people sing along to her popular songs until their voices are hoarse. This is not Kidane on stage – this is the Diva and I feel I understand her even though I have no words to express this understanding. The Diva and her all-male band – she thrives, loves being in control of all of them, all their macho selves held and sewn together by her voice.

Almost two hours into the concert – a song ends – she bows her head, and lifting only her eyes so that it looks like she is about to charge the crowd, she says, "I believe in God." I expect her to say she believes in the devil as well – but this is a different crowd – soldiers do not need to know the devil, the trenches are hell – they need to believe that they are fighting tyranny for democracy. This group of men yet to be wounded or killed, yet knowing that for some of them death is certain, and those who had survived and lost a limb or faith, and the relatives of those who died, they all need hope. They do not need to be reminded of the devil, they need to be reminded of God, of hope.

The band leaves the stage in silence. Mustafa comes and hands me an envelope. "She wants you to have this," he says as he sits by me. A choir dressed in blue comes in and standing in front of them is a *krar* player, short, and overweight. I open the envelope – it's a Tizita, in Amharic and in English. It's all written down by hand. I realize it was the Diva who has done the translation.

The *krar* starts off with a solo as she sways on the side, now more self-aware. She waits a little bit more and says something that Mustafa translates for me as 60,000 people get on their feet, yell, clap and shush each other. "It's a Tizita by Bezawork. She wants to pay homage to one of the greatest Tizita singers of all time," he translates. A few reps by the krar player, she closes her eyes and brings the microphone to her mouth, keeps swaying from side to side as if waiting for a cue that only she knows – I remember this from her performance at the ABC. The krar player's fingers at times a blur, at other times picking up one note after the other, keeps nodding in her direction, as if telling her, I am waiting for you, enter now.

60,000 people still on their feet waiting, and the waiting itself feels like a song. The choir sways with her waiting. The band members taking a break have also come out to the sides of the stage, a little worry and pride etched on their faces. And then whatever she was waiting for, perhaps a perfect balance between the krar and the loud anticipation from the crowd comes to pass. Her voice, hoarse from all the high charged singing earlier is cracked a bit but it adds to the music. I finally allow myself to look at the lyrics – they are in Amharic but I follow them listening to her voice not for words and their meaning, but as an instrument trying to tell us something. What does it matter what the words mean? I listen.

Hiiwot zora zora, TeQuma tizitan

Hiiwot zora zora, TeQuma tizitan

Dirron ayto madneQ, yesekenu eletta

Dirron ayto madneQ, yesekenu eletta

Deggun mastawesha, baynorewu tizita

Deggun mastawesha, baynorewu tizita

Negen baltemegnat, sewu . . . .

Negen baltemegnat, sewu . . . .

The cadence of her voice relaxed, the voice I know to be hers – it's almost like she is having a chat with the Tizita – her voice . . . the word I have been looking for comes to me – her androgynous voice rising falling with the bass and the krar, drawing out sorrow as if from a well – and when she repeats Tizita, Tizita, I hear split images of Bedele and her, alive and young and vital, the tragedy of what awaits their happiness in the horizon. Love and its mischief, it came and left, her voice the instrument cries.

Tizita bicha newu, yelib guadegna

Tizita bicha newu, yelib guadegna

Letamemech hiiwot, meTSnagna medagna

Letamemech hiiwot, meTSnagna medagna

The way her voice quivers, life has become unbearable, cannot be lived as is and something has to give . . .

Eyayun malefin, lemedelign aynein

Eyayun malefun, lemedelign aynein

Eyayu malefun, lemedelign aynein

What is she pleading for and whom is she imploring? Here I got lost in my own thoughts. The Diva, I know she can hit any note she wants – she had done it with me, just yesterday with her kids running around the yard, the sun that had just set an hour before glowing through the clouds. But this evening she is holding back, and where her voice takes command and soars, she flicks her hand up in the air as if to hold herself back, and she lets the krar play on eight or so beats before coming back to the song.

That gesture again and I put the lyrics down. I start to watch each time she raises her hand – the gesture elides over something. I watch hard enough to notice that she did that to pull herself back. The Corporal had done it, the holding back, at the ABC but not to the same effect as Kidane. We had been angry at his holding back because we wanted a bit of that flagellation that comes with facing one's demons – catharsis. But Kidane is getting rewarded – the crowd going crazy each time. The choir comes and completes the gesture by giving depth as opposed to height through a solo.

That gesture again! And then it hits me; the crowd was going crazy each time she held back. It was so simple it makes me want to cry. The reason why some preachers are better than others, or some poets better than others – they merely suggest and your fears or wants at their most absolute manifest themselves. I could tell myself she was performing – but performance as I understood it was about show, fireworks – performances were not supposed to be what Kidane was doing, merely suggesting, being content to suggest and let us do her work. I look at the lyrics.

Shimagilei Teffa, shibet ende'dirro

Shimagilei Teffa, shibet ende'dirro

Shimagilei Teffa, shibet ende'dirro

Shimagilei Teffa, shibet ende'dirro

Shimagilei Teffa, shibet ende'dirro

Shimagilei Teffa, shibet ende'dirro

Shimagilei Teffa, shibet ende'dirro

The choir comes in again, this time allowing each voice to be soothing yet almost distinct – I can hear twenty voices, all of them with something to say singing together – this loss, it's ours, it's not to be feared, it's to be embraced. It is in the loss that they find life, they play with their voices. And the Diva is somewhere in their voices; her voice strong and vulnerable, almost lost but at the same time carrying them all. And then they slow down and let the krar take the lead until it too slows down and the song and performance ends. The stage is rushed. I expect Mustafa to jump into action. He shrugs when I look at him.

"She is safest here – no one would dare touch her," he says to me.

I look again. Her fans are not rushing the stage to take a piece of her, to take a memento home; they are hurling love and kisses at her. Others rush and stand at a respectful distance – they just want to be close to her. So I ask him if he can translate as I ask the people who have overrun our little VIP section some questions, or rather one question – What is the Tizita to you? I pick the people randomly.

A schoolboy still in uniform – *it fills me with pride.*

A soldier – *it makes death feel warmer.* I ask him through Mustafa to explain a little bit more. *Death, we are all going to die – me, maybe in a war. The way she sings it? It makes me know I am part of life – and I will be remembered even after I am gone.*

A couple that wouldn't be able to hide their love for each other even if they tried – *If I was to lose her, I would kill myself* the man says.

And if he died, I would go on living – I would find the strength to live for the both of us – she says, laughs, and they try to make their way to the Diva.

An old white woman, high as a kite and dressed like a 1960s hippie – *The Tizita is a mirror that does not like one single thing.* I ask her to explain but she pinches me on my cheek playfully, like Miriam would do, and says, *live long enough son.*

An old man with his son – *my daughter died in the liberation war – I find comfort knowing I will join her soon.*

The son/brother – *The Tizita is the blood in our soil – the Tizita makes it boil.* I ask him to explain and he says he has no words beyond that.

Mustafa slaps me on my back – "And you my friend, what does the Tizita mean to you?"

I am taken aback by the question but also surprised by how readily the answer rolls off my tongue.

"Just how little of life I understand," I answer.

"And you?" I ask him.

He looks over at the Diva and I am almost afraid of what he will say.

"I would kill or die for her," he answers.

Frieda Ekotto

L'Art de Regarder: Une Lettre de Frieda Ekotto à Frida Khalo, The art of looking: A letter to Frida Kahlo from Frieda Ekotto

Translated by **Emily Goedde**

Quel Malheur que d'être femme ! Et pourtant le pire malheur, quand on est femme, est au fond de ne pas comprendre que c'en est un.

Kierkegaard

L'ART DE REGARDER

Une lettre de Frieda Ekotto à Frida Kahlo

Frida Kahlo n'est qu'émotion. Le propos de Kierkegaard ne correspond en rien à cette artiste unique en son genre. Elle s'est concentrée sur elle-même et sur ses sensations. Sans conteste, c'est la femme de mes désirs ! Elle laisse au monde un patrimoine pictural au travers duquel elle assume sa féminité jusqu'à son dernier souffle. Être femme pour Frida Kahlo ne fut pas un malheur, au contraire. Sur chaque photo, elle est habillée chic, elle est sereine, séduisante, prête à croquer et à être croquée. Comme toutes les femmes avec lesquelles je voudrais avoir une relation intime, j'ai honte de l'avouer, j'ai honte de me laisser aller, mais je les admire de loin et de près. Je n'ose pas dire : « Oui, je te désire, je te veux. » Je dis juste : « Oh ! Je veux... » Cette phrase est simple ou du moins, elle paraît facile à prononcer. Il y a une vraie pudeur qui m'envahit quand j'ouvre la bouche pour la proférer. Ce sont des choses qu'on ne dit pas, on les garde pour soi. C'est mon jardin secret. J'aurais sûrement tremblé devant elle comme je l'ai été devant ce grand poète des caraïbes Aimé Césaire. L'émotion !

Dans de moments de doute (comme celui-ci que je traverse), j'aurais voulu commencer cette lettre par une date précise inscrite dans le calendrier. Quelque chose comme ce qui suit : « Frida Kahlo et Frieda Ekotto se sont connues en 1986 dans son musée de la Casa Azul à Coyoacán au Mexique. Quelle belle couleur que cette maison bleue où vit encore aujourd'hui une mémoire, une vie, l'œuvre d'une peintre qui brise l'âme par la profondeur de son expression artistique ! Partout des peintures impressionnantes, d'admirables portraits et autoportraits, ses robes colorées, son beau visage, ses yeux qui me parlent, mais aussi des odeurs, la sensation d'une vie brisée par la désolation. L'effet Frida Kahlo, depuis mon séjour mexicain qui date de mes années d'études se poursuit, s'amplifie, se transforme, rebondit et me poursuit. Elle est partout et nulle part. Elle est un effet de vérité sur l'histoire de mes parents, et de mon pays le Cameroun. Tout le monde semble la connaître, et surtout sa vie de femme à travers une relation complexe, à l'instar de cet autre grand peintre Diego Rivera, sa grenouille adorée.

Or, moi, je la connais de l'intérieur. C'est à travers elle que j'ai commencé à aimer mon nom. Ce prénom si doux glisse entre les lèvres. Or, Frida Kahlo est un nom historique, mais pour moi, c'est d'abord une femme porteuse d'histoire, de politique, de philosophie et une peintre unique voire *une femme exceptionnelle* comme l'annonçait la bande publicitaire du film *Frida* de Julie Taymor (2002). Je voudrais la toucher, glisser ma main sur ses joues, effleurer son nez, laisser mes doigts monter et descendre sur les siennes. J'aime les mains des artistes. Je suis toujours très émue quand je touche les mains d'un de mes amis écrivains. Ses doigts sont fins, longs, attirants. Certes, pour Frida Kahlo, je meurs d'envie de sentir ses nymphes avec le bout de mon index. Frida, je t'aurais aimé comme une femme aime une autre femme. Je t'aime si loin, si près de ta peinture. Tu as vu le jour avant moi, je suis dans la nuit avec toi et demain, je verrai le jour. Demain, tu me regarderas avec le même regard du portrait que j'ai choisi de mettre dans mon bureau. C'est une photo en noir et blanc, tu es belle Frida Kahlo et je t'admire. Un cillement de l'œil sur ta peinture donne de l'intensité à ma poitrine comme si elle arrachait mon cœur. Tes peintures circulent à travers le monde. Chacune d'elles est différente, une émotion particulière, quelque chose de très touchant, ma chère Frida. Quelle émotion, ton art ! Là, tu y déposes ta souffrance, ton humanité.

On les aime, on les admire, on peut même y toucher ou sentir cette douleur qui te terrassait sur ton lit d'hôpital des années durant. On apprécie surtout ta féminité exubérante, tes belles robes assorties aux colliers magnifiques. On entend presque leur timbre, mais la dernière scène où elle se fait transporter dans son lit de malade pour se célébrer dans cette galerie où son mari Diego et les autres admirent son travail, elle débarque avec son lit dans une robe aux couleurs vives, elle est pleine de vie, elle est *Frida* comme dirait

Baudelaire, il s'agit de « la célébration de quelque mystère douloureux. » De la voir s'animer dans son lit, on oublie qu'elle est malade, mourante à la limite. L'enthousiasme de cette femme rappelle que la vie n'est que regard et passion.

Ce qu'elle est, Frida Kahlo l'est tout d'abord en vertu non d'un destin, fatalité cosmique, volonté divine ou nature déterminée, mais d'une histoire. Et dans cette histoire, on ne saurait l'enfermer comme dans une limite contraignante et indépassable. Son être et son œuvre éclatent dans toutes sortes de postures possibles, insaisissables tout autant qu'affirmation de soi. Je suis Frida Kahlo. *Soy yo* !

Je reviens à nouveau au Mexique. Cette fois avec Frida Kahlo, peintre allemande et mexicaine. J'arrive trop tard, car elle n'y est plus, seule sa peinture continue de m'éblouir. Sublime, cette femme qui a tant souffert dans sa chair. Comment la repenser, comment l'extraire du silence de mon âme ? L'accident de voiture où elle a failli perdre la vie. L'accident de voiture où j'ai aussi failli perdre la vie. À cinq ans, je perds mes camarades d'école dans un accident mortel. Mon père vient récupérer mon cadavre comme d'autres parents. Or moi, je suis dans les décombres à la recherche de mon cartable. J'avais un joli petit cartable cuir marron. Il se trouve à présent dans les objets que ma famille collectionne passionnément, telle une relique. Fort ému, à la soutenance de ma thèse, mon père raconte cette histoire les larmes aux yeux. « Ma fille, Frieda, ma Sulamithe, ma mère est née avec une étoile lumineuse, elle a déjà frisé la mort plusieurs fois. C'est un miracle qu'elle soit là aujourd'hui, qu'elle soutienne sa thèse sur un criminel, Jean Genet, un lumineux comme elle, ça ne me surprend pas du tout. »

Au cœur de cette histoire d'amour platonique s'entrecroisent celle de nos deux pays et celle aussi de nos pères : L'Allemagne et le Cameroun. Inutile de revenir sur ce malheur, il n'empêche : le prénom Frida/Frieda est la marque pour chacune de nous d'une blessure profonde. Ce qui m'intéresse dans l'itinéraire de ces prénoms, c'est leur affrontement à l'Histoire. Frida Kahlo, qui devrait être l'Allemagne même, s'y oppose. Frieda Ekotto accepte l'Allemagne, qui lui donne une assise, du leste. L'histoire coloniale nous tatoue jusque sous la peau. Certes, j'ai aujourd'hui le choix de refuser ce prénom. Je pourrai me faire appeler Sula, c'est court, c'est direct, c'est doux à prononcer. Su-la contient deux sons comme d'ailleurs Frie-da.

Je suis née au Cameroun d'une mère Congolaise et d'un père Camerounais. Je viens à la rencontre de la grande majesté Kahlo avec mon passé dominé. Les Allemands occupent le Cameroun. Notre histoire commune commence en 1885 autour d'une table en Allemagne avec les dignitaires de tous les pays européens pour le dépeçage de l'Afrique : aucun Africain n'est présent parmi eux. Que dois-je donc penser moi de cette division ? Aujourd'hui la retombée de ce grand conciliabule est ce prénom que je traîne comme un boulet. Car, même au Cameroun, la nouvelle génération ne sait plus que notre pays a été une possession allemande. J'ai appris à aimer ce prénom parce que toi aussi tu le portais. Mais quel poids ! 1885, la Conférence de Berlin : le but est simple, se partager la partie subsaharienne de l'Afrique. Partout l'inscription de la violence, partout l'horreur qui nous meurtrit chacune dans son coin. Un point commun : l'Allemagne de Bismarck. Frida, j'aurais tellement aimé te parler de cette histoire, de notre histoire. J'imagine aisément tes réponses à mes questions. Je sais que tu regarderais le contour de mes lèvres sensuelles. Le collier rouge que je porte aujourd'hui aurait attiré ton regard. Tu l'aurais trouvé joli et tu m'aurais fait un clin d'œil. Ta passion, ton génie, ton désir pour ce Diego qui s'enflammait au quart de tour au contact des corps. Il baisait toutes les femmes qui passaient sous ses yeux, y compris ta propre sœur. Toi, Frida, tu as réagi en femme jalouse, tu as quitté ta grenouille adorée, enfin ! Mais la vie vous avait scellé et cela personne n'y pouvait rien. Il est revenu dans ta vie comme ton deuxième mari. Ce petit gros talentueux, un être impossible, vivant sa vie d'artiste, oubliant que toi aussi tu n'avais qu'une envie de vivre cette vie avec lui. Ton œuvre artistique est aussi importante que la sienne. Ce n'était pas cela la donne. Là, tu as eu quelques relations avec de jolies femmes, Frida ! Je sais, c'est le désir, n'est-ce pas ? Tes caresses sur leurs fesses, tes baisers doux, humides, tièdes, chauds, ta langue sur leurs seins, ton parfum de femme. Oh ! Frida, ton regard, trop profond, je le sens sur moi, discrètement. Je reste figée dans un coin et je t'observe jouir avec elles.

Nous sommes dans l'Histoire. Je parle du passé au présent, du présent au passé. Tout se mélange, mais tout reste clair aussi. Frida Kahlo, c'est toi la femme que je désire ou disons que j'aurais voulu avoir dans mon lit. Ce n'est pas vulgaire ce que je dis là, en somme, c'est un peu de l'ordre du sacré, cette femme qu'on idéalise de loin, dans l'Histoire . . . Que nous dit l'Histoire ? Pour Frida, une passion violente, une souffrance infinie. Quelle souffrance, mes aïeuls. Ce monde de mensonges dans lequel nous vivons. Au moins Frida, tu avais ta peinture, tes pinceaux sont des armes révolutionnaires ou comme dirait le poète Césaire, tes armes miraculeuses !

Frida Kahlo, je me demande encore comment te dire que je suis dans ton ombre, petite, mais pharaonique, car je t'élève dans la profondeur d'un baiser de femme, dans la douceur de ma caresse. Il y a un portrait de toi dans mes bureaux, dans ma chambre, dans mon bureau à la maison. Tu es dans ma vie, tu es importante pour moi, tu me signales ta grandeur, ta dignité, ta passion, ta créativité. Dans le quotidien, dans ma philosophie du moment, du maintenant, je te vois me regardant, me souriant, me donnant ton soutien. Je sais que tu es là sur ce chemin compliqué du quotidien, que tu m'acceptes comme je suis avec toutes mes contradictions. Toi-même, tu avais une montagne de contradictions. Vivre veut dire passer des compromis et comprendre les contradictions qui nous définissent. Je ne saurais me lever sans ton soutien. Quand il m'arrive d'oublier qui je suis, je souffle un peu, je me conte et me raconte, comme me le recommande Marthe, ma compagne.

J'ai décidé de raconter ma relation avec toi. Mais tu sais, Frida Kahlo, tu sais que je me demande souvent qui je suis. J'avance dans l'ombre, doucement, en cherchant une lumière pour m'énoncer, me guider. Hier, j'ai parlé avec mon grand ami Nimrod sur qui je suis. Il me parle de la limite de la paranoïa. J'ai un peu peur, peur de me savoir peut-être malade. J'ai peur . . . je sais que Rimbaud l'a dit : « Je est un autre. » Est-ce mon cas ? J'aime parler avec cet ami, c'est doux, c'est tendre, c'est passionnant. La question de la vérité reste une idée majeure dans la vie. Le dire vrai, être vrai, ne pas se mentir. Se laisser vivre dans ce monde qui m'échappe, mais auquel je dois faire face. Toi, Frida, je sais combien tu as souffert, combien tu te battais pour dépasser cette souffrance physique de par ton accident, mais aussi cette souffrance psychologique, tu voulais être mère. Je sais que toi, dans ta maison, tu avais des enfants, beaucoup d'enfants qui venaient se nourrir chez toi, qui venaient te donner ce sourire que tu recherchais chez un enfant. Comme moi, tu as eu des enfants, ceux des autres. Moi, je ne suis pas mère non plus. J'ai juste élevé quatre enfants laissés par ma feue sœur Mirabelle. Je suis quand même mère par procuration, mais pas comme tu le voulais toi . . . Mais je sais que tu as donné beaucoup d'amour aux enfants, à tes enfants, aux enfants qui venaient manger chez maman Frida. Tu les attendais tous les jours. Ils arrivaient bruyants, pleins d'un bonheur qui te comblait.

Dans mon imaginaire, tu es une grande femme, un amour, une passion ; l'inspiration, je la puise en toi et ton œuvre. Enfin, Hector Biancioti me donne les outils pour faire tomber le « e » de mon prénom. C'est dans son fauteuil que va s'asseoir Dany Laferrière, cet écrivain haïtien avec lequel j'ai eu le plaisir de travailler pendant mes premières années d'enseignement. J'aimais ces cours où il tenait des conversations complètement décousues avec les étudiants. Biancioti disait que ce qui l'a décidé à abandonner l'espagnol pour le français, c'est le *e muet* français. En italien tout comme en espagnol, la voyelle muette n'existe pas. Le jour où Biancioti a savouré la lune au lieu de *luna*, cela fut pour lui une grande découverte. Or que découvrit-il ? Le silence. Et que découvrir avec Frida Kahlo ? La fureur qui fait voler en éclat le « e » muet ! Plus précisément, son inutile inscription. Mais est-elle si inutile que ça ? Rien n'est moins sûr ! Le *i* de Frida est long, il sert à prolonger la voyelle de ce joli nom ! Tout comme le *h* de Kahlo. Chaque langue a son génie propre pour faire sonner les mots. La génétique textuelle n'est jamais transcodable telle quelle d'une langue à l'autre. Mais tu n'es pas femme à procéder avec prudence. Pourtant, tu n'es pas imprudente. Frida est désormais un prénom hispanique, telle est ton éclatante victoire, à l'égale de ta planétaire renommée !

Je t'adore, calorifique Frida Kahlo ! Ta Frieda Ekotto !

> *What a misfortune to be a woman! And yet, for a woman the worst misfortune is to fundamentally not understand that she is one.*
>
> <u>Kierkegaard</u>

THE ART OF LOOKING

A letter by Frieda Ekotto to Frida Khalo

Frida Kahlo is sheer emotion. Kierkegaard's comment has nothing to do with her, this artist, unlike any other. She concerned herself with her being and her feelings. There's no question: I desire her. She left behind a pictorial legacy in which she grappled with her femininity until her dying breath. For Frida Kahlo, to be a woman wasn't a misfortune, quite the opposite. In every photo, she is dressed stylishly; she is serene, seductive, ready to devour and be devoured. As with every woman with whom I'd like to be intimate, I'm ashamed to admit it, ashamed to say too much, but I admire them both close up and from afar. I don't dare say, "I desire you. I want you." So I simply say, "Oh, I want . . ." It's a simple phrase, easy enough to say. There is this pudeur when I open my mouth, when I say it. These things are not said. We keep them to ourselves. This is my secret garden. I would have surely trembled before her like I did before the great Caribbean poet Aimé Césaire. Passion!

In moments of doubt (like the one I'm having right now), I would have liked to start with an exact date. Something like: "Frida Kahlo and Frieda Ekotto met in 1986 at the Casa Azúl in Coyoacán, Mexico." What a beautiful color, the blue of this house, which today still holds a remembrance, a life, a painter's work that crushes the soul with the depth of its artistic expression. Breathtaking paintings are everywhere, exemplary portraits and self-portraits, her colored dresses, her beautiful face, her eyes that speak to me, but also the smells, the feeling of a life crushed by desolation. Since this stay in Mexico during my college years, the Frida Kahlo effect has continued to grow, to transform, to twist and turn and haunt me. She is everywhere and nowhere. She is an element of truth among the story of my family and my country, Cameroon. Everyone seems to know her, especially her experience as a woman involved in a complicated relationship with that other great painter, Diego Rivera, her beloved frog.

As for me, I know her from the inside. It's through her that I began to love my name. My given name, which slides so sweetly between the lips. It's true that Frida Kahlo is a historic name, although for me, she is first and foremost a female bearer of the historical, the political, the philosophical, and a singular painter, in other words an *exceptional woman*, as the teaser for Julie Taymor's film *Frida* (2002) puts it. I would like to touch her, to run my hand across her cheek, to brush her nose, to let my fingers climb up and down hers. I love artists' hands. Something in me is moved when I touch my writer friends' hands. Their long, fine, beautiful fingers. I'll admit it. I'm dying to touch Frida Kahlo's labia with the tip of my index. Frida, I would have loved to love you like a woman loves another woman. I love you so close, so far from your painting. You saw the light of day before me, and I am in the night with you and tomorrow I will see the day. Tomorrow you will look at me with that look you have in the portrait I chose for my office. It's a black-and-white photograph. You are the beautiful Frida Kahlo and I am your admirer. A glance at your painting makes me feel as if my heart were being torn from my chest. Your paintings travel the world. Each is different, with its particular emotion, infinitely touching, my dear Frida. What passion, your art, there where you placed your suffering, your humanity.

They are loved, admired. The pain that left you prostrate on your hospital bed for years at a time can even be touched or felt. We admire your exuberant femininity, your many beautiful dresses and magnificent necklaces. We can almost hear them tinkling, as in that the last scene, when she has herself carried in on her sick bed to be celebrated in the gallery. As her husband Diego and the others express their admiration, she appears upon her bed in a brightly colored dress, full of life. She is *Frida* as Baudelaire would have put it, "the celebration of some painful mystery." Lying on her bed, her face aglow, we forget she is ill, practically dying. Her enthusiasm reminds us that life is nothing but passion and vision.

Whatever she is, Frida Kahlo is first and foremost a result not of destiny, cosmic bad luck, divine will or natural causes, but of a history, a story. And in this history, story, it is impossible to hold her fast within restrictive, impassable limits. Her being and her oeuvre explode into all kinds of possible points of view, which are elusive even as they are affirmations of self. I am Frida Kahlo. *Soy yo!*

I return again to Mexico. This time with Frida Kahlo, German and Mexican painter. I arrive too late, for she is no longer there, only her paintings, which continue to dazzle me, remain. Sublime, this woman who suffered so in her flesh. How to think of her anew, how to extract her from the silence of my soul? The car accident in which she almost died. The car accident in which I too almost died. Five years old, I lose my classmates in a fatal accident. My father comes with the other parents to claim the bodies. But I am in the wreckage looking for my schoolbag. I had a pretty brown leather satchel. We have it still, a relic among the other objects my family so passionately collects. My father was so moved at my dissertation defense, that he told this story with tears in his eyes. "My daughter Frieda, my Sulamithe, my mother was born beneath a bright star. She has been close to death more than once. It's a miracle that she is here today. It does not surprise me at all that she is defending her dissertation on the criminal Jean Genet, a bright star like herself."

Intertwined at the heart of this platonic love story are those of our countries and our fathers: Germany and Cameroon. It's pointless to revisit this misfortune. There's no reason to—the name Frida/Frieda marks the depths of our wounds. What interests me is our name's trajectories, their confrontations with History. Frida Kahlo, who should be Germany itself, is opposed to it. Frieda Ekotto accepts Germany, which gave her a foundation, a ballast. Colonial history tattoos us beneath our very skin. Indeed, I could now reject this name. I have the choice. I could call myself Sula, it's short, it's direct, it's easy to say. It even has two syllables like Frie-da.

I was born in Cameroon to a Congolese mother and a Cameroonian father. I come to my encounter with Kahlo, Her Grand Majesty, with my dominated past. The Germans occupied Cameroon. Our common history starts in 1885 around a table in Germany with dignitaries from each European country present and ready to carve up Africa. There was not a single African. So what should I think of this division? Today the consequences of this great secret meeting is this name I drag around like a millstone. For, even in Cameroon, the new generation no longer knows our country was a German possession. I learned to love this name because you, too, carried it. But what weight! 1885, the Berlin Conference. The goal is simple: to divvy up sub-Saharan Africa. Everywhere the inscription of violence; everywhere the horror that wounds each where she is. A common point: Bismarck's Germany. Frida, I would so much have liked to talk with you about this history, our history. I can easily imagine how you would respond to my questions. I know you would study the contours of my sensual lips. That the red necklace I'm wearing today would attract your attention. You would have liked it and you would have winked at me. Your passion, your genius, your desire for Diego who set your body on fire the moment your bodies touched. He kissed all the women who passed beneath his eyes, including your very own sister. You, Frida, you reacted as a jealous woman, you left your beloved frog, finally! But life had fastened you together, and there was nothing anyone could do. He returned to your life like a second husband. That fat, talented, little man, an impossible being, living his life of an artist, forgetting that you, too, had only one desire: to live that life with him. Your artistic oeuvre is as important as his. But that was not the deal. So you found some pretty women, Frida! I know. It's desire, non? Your caresses on their buttocks, your soft kisses, wet, warm, hot, your tongue on theirs, your female perfume. Oh! Frida, your look, too deep. I feel it upon me, discreetly. I sit frozen in a corner and watch you enjoy yourself.

We are within History. I speak of the past in the present, of the present in the past. Everything mixes together but still remains clear. Frida Kahlo, I desire you, or let's just say I would like to have you in my bed. I'm not being vulgar, this belongs to the realm of the sacred, this woman idealized from afar, in History . . . . what we call History? For Frida, a violent passion, infinite suffering. What suffering, my ancestors. This world of lies in which we live. At least, Frida, you had your painting, your brushes, your revolutionary weapons, or as the poet Césaire said, your miraculous weapons!

Frida Kahlo, I ask myself still how to tell you that I am in your small but pharaonic shadow, for I raise you in the depth of a woman's kiss, in the softness of my caresses. There is a picture of you in my office, in my room, in my office at home. You are in my life, you are important to me. You remind me of your grandeur, your dignity, your passion, your creativity. In the everyday, in my philosophy of the moment, of the now, I see you look at me, smile at me, supporting me. I know that you are there on the complicated path of the everyday, that you accept me as I am with all my contradictions. You, too, were a mountain of contradictions. To want to live means to compromise and to understand the contradictions that define us. I wouldn't know how to get out of bed without your support. When I forget who I am, I breathe a little, and I speak to myself again and again, as Marthe, my partner, recommends I do.

I decided to speak about my relationship with you. But you know, Frida Kahlo, you know that I ask myself often who I am. I move forward in the shadows, slowly, looking for a light to clarify me, to guide me. Yesterday, I spoke with my good friend Nimrod about who I am. He spoke to me about the limits of paranoia. I'm a little frightened, afraid others might think I'm sick. I'm afraid. . . . I know Rimbaud said it, "I is an other." Is this true for me? I love talking with Nimrod. He is gentle, tender, passionate. The question of truth remains an important idea in life. To speak the truth, to be true, not to lie to oneself. To let oneself live in this world which eludes me but which I must face. You, Frida, I know how much you suffered, how much you fought to overcome the physical suffering from your accident, but also psychological suffering, you wanted to be a mother. I know that you, in your house, you had children, many children who came for nourishment, who came to give you the smiles you sought in children, other people's children. Me, I am not a mother either. I only raised my late sister Mirabelle's four children, so I am mother by proxy, not as you wanted to be. . . . But I know that you gave so much love to your children, to the children who came to eat at Mamá Frida's house. You waited for them every day. They were rowdy and filled with a joy that delighted you.

In my imagination you are a great woman, a love, a passion; inspiration, I draw from you and your oeuvre. In the end, Hector Bianciotti gives me the tools to drop the "e" from my name, from in his Académie seat, which the Haitian writer Dany Laferrière will come to fill, and with whom I had the pleasure of working during my first years of teaching. I loved his courses consisting of completely disjointed conversations with students. Bianciotti said that the reason he decided to give up Spanish for French was the French *silent e*. In Italian, like in Spanish, there are no silent vowels. For Bianciotti the day he learned to savor *la lune* in the place of *la luna* was one of great discovery. What did he discover? Silence. And what to discover with Frida Kahlo? The fury that explodes in that silent "e"! More precisely, the uselessness of writing it. But is it so useless? Not necessarily! The *i* in Frida is long—it's there to prolong the vowel in this lovely name! Just like the *h* in Kahlo. Each language has its genius for making words sing. Textual genetics is never transcodable from one language to another. But you're not a woman to do things prudently. Although you're not imprudent, either. Frida is henceforth a Latina name, as is your brilliant victory, your planetary fame!

I adore you, my arousing, enkindling Frida Kahlo,
Your Frieda Ekotto

Translator's note

"Frida Kahlo n'est qu'émotion." This first sentence is, naturally, one of the hardest in the piece to translate. The ones that seem simple often are. It isn't a question of grammar. It translates fairly directly into "Frida Kahlo is naught but," if you want to be archaic about it. Or "Frida Kahlo is only," if you want to put a more positive spin on the exclusionary aspect of "n'est que." The difficulty lies elsewhere, in the subtle differences between the cognates *émotion* and *emotion*.

The formidable French dictionary *Larousse* defines *émotion* as: "Trouble subit, agitation passagère causés par un sentiment vif de peur, de surprise, de joie, etc.," which we could render as "sudden disturbance, temporary state of agitation caused by a strong feeling of fear, surprise, joy, etc." (here, too, we have a tricky cognate in "trouble"). *The New Oxford American Dictionary*, however, establishes *emotion* as "a natural instinctive state of mind deriving from one's circumstances, mood, or relationships with others." These two definitions allow us to begin to sense some differences. The French emphasizes the passing affect of strong feelings, while the English is focused on a state of mind or mood. In this way, *émotion* reads more as an active reaction rather than a state of being influenced by circumstance. For our sentence, this means that Frida is not so much "naught but a state of mind," but rather the "pure, active harnessing of intense feeling or sensation."

These subtle differences are what we learn from the translation process. They're the reason translation notes like these are (in my opinion) so fascinating. They are opportunities to observe what can be gained and learned as we move between languages, considering a vast Venn diagram of interlingual synonyms and metonyms. This expansive space translation creates is not often apparent in the final translated product, however, and is often further obfuscated by criticism that focuses upon lack or poor choices, rather than considering each translation's particular arc of meaning.

For me, it isn't translation that's lacking, but the discourse to acknowledge what is generated in the process. Because in the end, we have to make a choice. Among the many possible words and phrases, which glow before me in their Venn diagram glory, how am I going to translate "Frida Kahlo n'est qu'émotion"?

"Frida Kahlo is sheer emotion." This way keeps the strong syntactic and rhythmic simplicity of Ekotto's sentence, but uses "sheer" to emphasize *émotion*'s intensity and force. (When *émotion* appears elsewhere in the essay, I've chosen to translate it as "passion.") What do you think? What does the space between languages, created in the process of translation, evoke for you?

– Emily Goedde

Susan Kiguli

Omuti, The Tree |
Nnakazzadde, Mother |
Wayirindi, The Plague |
The Unending Game,
Omuzannyo Ogutakoma

Translated by **Merit Kabugo**

OMUTI[1]

Ahaha sooka olabe omuti bwe gwettika
Obukoola lukunkumuli
N'enkuyanja y'ennyembe

N'obunyonyi obw'omu bire
Kw'ossa okwo n'ebisu byabwo
Labayo bwe gwettika
Waggulu ne gwettika
Ne wansi ne gwebagajja emirandira gyagwo
Wamma omuti ggwo gwayitawo.

Wabula waliyo ababbuukirira

Mbu tippa eza loole
Mbu nazo zettika nnyo
Kafankunaali w'abantu
Babuwe ne zikubako enfaafa y'ebintu
Wabbuto n'abwegera
Naye leka leka wamma
Kuba yo tippa oluusi
Egenda mu kkubo eyiwaayiwako

Ate nno ka nkubbireko
Olumu bagiziyizaako

Nti leero eneesomba wali ow'a Katale ak'e Nsambya

THE TREE

Ooh! Behold, what a tree can carry!
Millions of leaves
Multitudes of succulent mangoes

As well as little birds of the sky
And their nests, too
Behold, what a tree can carry
On its head, it carries
On its feet, it heaves and carries its roots
Indeed the tree surpasses all.

But there are those who are voluble

Who argue that lorry trucks
Are also such big carriers
Of tonnes of all kinds of goods
They brim over with countless goods
And the stomachs bulge
But wait a minute
The truck, on occasions
spills some of the baggage along the way

Let me tell you a little secret
Sometimes the truck's workload is regulated

Deciding that today the truck Will only carry goods at Nsambya market

---

[1] The original versions of the poems "Omuti | The Tree," "Nnakazzadde | Mother," "Wayirindi | The Plague" were written in Luganda.

Aaah kati tulabe wamma	*Come on, let us plan properly*
Waliyo amayinja gali ku kasozi	*There are those slates*
Namungoona.	*At Namungoona hill.*

Naye era eyawa omuti ebbeetu — *But the one who gave liberty to the tree*

Bannange yasukkuluma — *Transcends all*
Akeera maliiri n'alagira — *He wakes up early to give instructions*

Nti obukoola bwa leero — *Ordering that this time*
Bulina kuba butono ate nga — *The leaves must be small in size*

Bwasongolerera — *And pointed in shape*
Ate oba okyali awo — *While you are still mesmerized*
Okutunula ennyo nga bwa bigondogondo. — *A second look reveals that they are variegated.*
Kw'ossa buli baaba obulinga — *And ooh! There are those that look like*

Obulina ebisukko ne kakugwaako — *They have lesions and if they fall on your skin*

Anti ggwe ne weyagula — *you desperately scratch yourself*
Wabula kyokka kkiriza — *You really need to acknowledge*
Omuti ggwo gwayitawo — *That the tree surpasses all*
Era alosa omuti kyokka — *And whoever gives life to the tree*

Ye yasukkuluma n'akamala. — *Is indeed an invincible force.*

NNAKAZZADDE   *MOTHER*

Leero ebigambo ntambudde na bisengejje
Mbisengeka mbisengejja saagala kuwammanta

Today I have moved with filtered words
I pattern and sieve them because I do not want to grope for words

Kale nze nteesa buteesa nti nnakazadde awaanwako
Kisaana okusaasaanya omuwendo gwa maama
Teriiyo aliguvuganya.

I come with a simple proposal that a mother deserves praise
The value of a mother needs to be broadcast
The value of a mother is indisputable.

Kyokka kyo kya mazima ye maama ayatiikirira
Era singa nsobola bannyabo nandibatadde wamu
Olwo ne nsooka nsaba Nnamugereka angerekere ku mmunyeenye ze.

It is indeed true that a mother is an icon
If it were possible, I would bring all mothers together
I would then pray to the Almighty to bequeath some of His stars to me.

Kuba ddala nandiddidde eddaala ne nninya ne nnona
Ku ziri ezimyansa mwattu buli omu ne muwaako emu
Ate oba nandisabye Omutonzi n'anjazika ku langi eza musoke
Bambi buli omu ne muwaako emu.

I would then get a ladder and climb up the sky
To pick some of the twinklers and hand one to each mother
Or I would ask the creator to lend me some of the colors of the rainbow
Then I would give a color to each of the mothers.

Kuba bambi omukwano gwa maama simanyi ani aligwogerako.

Because I am not sure whether anyone can ever fully express a mother's love.

WAYIRINDI	*THE PLAGUE*
Wayirindi, otwerigombeddeko nno!	*Plague, you have indeed trampled on us!*
Ani yakuwa olukusa okwekkusa otyo?	*Who permitted you to be such a glutton?*
Oddidde ebyali ebitiibwa obitimbye okwo	*What was once respectable*
Ku bisenge ebimogofu	*You now hang up on gaping walls*
Olwo osiita ng'asiika ebinyeebwa ebisiriira	*You are as mischievous as one scorching peanuts while roasting them*
Nti bwe binaggya tunaggyako ebikuta!	*Anticipating to skin the nuts after the roast!*
Otukongoodde ate n'otubaaga	*You have bullied and skinned us*
Olinga kamunye alengedde enkoko enjeru?	*You are like an eagle that has spotted a white chicken?*
Wayirindi otwerigombeddeko nnyo!	*Plague, you have indeed trampled on us!*
Essungu oliggye wa eryo?	*Why all that rage?*
N'obwebweena n'obwerippye mu lubuto?	*You even devour little ones clinging to the womb!*
Ne weddiza obukoko	*You snatch the chickens*
N'obatika obubuzi	*You stuff your cheeks with the goats*
Ne mu ggana n'oweekamu ennume?	*In a herd, you pick the bull?*
N'obusolo ku ttale	*Including game in the jungle*
Okudaala n'okirako abazadde ku mbaga	*You brag like parents at a child's wedding*
Nti atalina aweeke ejjinja	*Who urge the childless to babysit a stone*

Wayirindi otwerigombeddeko nnyo!	*Plague, you have indeed trampled on us!*
Obadde otya atalina nsonyi?	*Why are you so shameless?*
Ku buko otwala nsonzi	*You carry little tiny fish to your inlaws*
Nti yii ekyennyanja kyayinga obuwoomi!	*Claiming that fish is such a delicacy!*
Otulanga ki atubunya obufo?	*What do we owe you that you harass us so?*
Ebiwoobe bifuuse eby'olulango	*Weeping is such a common sight*
Olwo okubye akakule akatalaba mujja	*With your cynical laughter, as loud as that of a co-wife*
Nti he n'oyo anaafumba!	*Who belittles a new co-wife!*
Wayirindi otwerigombeddeko luno!	*Plague, you have indeed trampled on us!*
Naye naffe tunaakukwata bulago	*But we shall take you by the neck*
Tunaasooba nga nnawolovu alabye enswera	*We shall sneak on you like a chameleon catching a fly*
Tunaabanga Nakibinge nti n'emmuli zinaalwana	*Like Prince Nakibinge of old, we shall use even reeds to fight*
Anti baalugera nti okwerinda.	*Like the adage goes, be on your guard.*

THE UNENDING GAME[2]

We are at it again.
No one deserves to lose
A son, a father, a brother, a nephew, an uncle
A daughter, a mother, a sister, a niece, an aunt
No one.

No one deserves news
That a rock full of hatred hit her husband
That he writhed in blood

As television cameras rolled

No one merits public humiliation
With legs thrashing about

And foam at his mouth
While television cameras roll.

No one.

No one deserves to receive news of
The death of a father
By watching uniformed men

Club his head

Until he crumbles in an

OMUZANNYO OGUTAKOMA

Tuguzzeemu nate.
Tewali asaana kufiirwa
Mutabani, kitaawe, mugandawe, kizibwe, oba kojja
Muwalawe, nnyina, mwannyina, nnyazaala we, oba ssenga
Tewali n'omu.

Tewali asaana kuwulira
Nti ejjinja ericuuma obukyayi lyakubye bba
Nti bba yalaajanidde mu kitaba ky'omusaayi
Ng'abentambi za ttivvi beetala okumulaga

Tewali asaana kuweebuulwa atyo
Ng'amagulu ge gagudde nnagalaale

Ng'abimbye n'ejjovu mu kamwa
Ng'eno ab'entambi za ttivvi beetala okumulaga.

Tewali n'omu.

Tewali asaana kubikirwa

Nti kitawo yafudde
Ng'alaba abenaanise ebibomboola

Bakuba omwagalwa we entolima ku mutwe
Okutuusa lw'agaŋŋalama

---

[2] This poem is originally written in English.

Incoherent heap	N'afuuka omutulumbi
While television cameras run.	Ng'eno ab'entambi za ttivvi beetala.
No one.	Tewali n'omu.
No one deserves to see	Tewali asaana kutunuulira
Bullets lodged	Amasasi nga gasindirirwa
In the womb of their	Mu lubuto lwa muwala waabwe
Pregnant daughter	Eyetisse enda/ettu
Her clothes shredded	Engoye ze nga zisensulwa
By the power of violence and silence of terror.	Mu bikolwa eby'obukambwe n'ettima.
No one deserves knowledge of	Tewali asaana kumanya
Never knowing why such anger	Lwaki tamanyi lwaki obukambwe nga buno
Moves in loaded guns	Butambulira mu mmundu ezijjudde amasasi
No one.	Tewali n'omu.
No one deserves to travel long distances	Tewali asaana kuseyeggera ŋŋendo
To fetch the body of a child	Okuwondera omulambo gw'omwana
Sent to university in hope of glory	Eyagenda ku yunivasite afuuke ekkula
Because a bullet was lodged in	Kubanga yakubiddwa essasi ku mutwe
His head by a security guard	Nga liva ku mukuumi eyabadde
Who has lost the sense of foolish daring youth	Tamanyi kalaaca ka bavubuka
No one deserves this deliberate extravaganza	Tewali asaanira ffujjo lino lya lugenderezo

Of robbing life	*Effujjo ery'okutirimbula abantu*
Knowing it will be news for a day	*Ng'oli akimanyi nti gajja kuba mawulire ga kiseera buseera*
Then another folly will take over	*Olwo ate wajjewo kazoole omulala*
As families struggle with sorrow	*Ng'abantu balumwa obugigi olw'ennaku*
With furious young people	*Ng'abaana bakula n'obusungu obuzibu*
Growing up	*Nga bambi bajjudde ekiruyi*
To wreck their own nation	*Eky'okutaagula eggwanga lyabwe*
Which they disown everyday	*Eggwanga lye begaana buli lukya*
While they live in it	*So ng'ate babeera mu lyo*
Which they desire to flee	*Naye nga baagala okulyabulira*
Recognizing they cannot leave	*Bwe bakizuula nti tebasobola kuliviira*
Realising they are knotted up	*Ne bamanya nti balippiddwa muli*
in balls of rage and love	*Mu bituttwa by'obusungu n'omukwano*
Unable to disentangle.	*Mwe batakyasobola kwetakkuluza.*

Afua Ansong

"The Earth Is Heavy/ Holds Weight" "Drum" "Ananse's Web"

Translated by the author[1]

---

[1] The following poems are from Afua Ansong's Adinkra symbols in translation series

[Nsa'a- money collected from family members and friends to help cover the cost of burying one's dead. Asaawa-Cotton balls inserted into the nostrils of the dead to absorb fluids.
Note: In North America and Barbados, African women who were enslaved from West Africa were the largest harvesters of cotton.]

Mother, what have we done with earth's flower?
forcing it into holes of the dead
and wrapping it around cold limbs
not to warm but to exchange for coins and grief.
We laugh with the white man who drags
our hands into the deep soils until we are hoes
turning the calm of earth.

This cotton pulls children out of our bellies
to chains their nakedness.
This cotton is the labor of our fingers
we hide under our beds and uncover again
to weave a dress, to cover the holes in our skin.
This cotton drives away our angels
and brings near spirits with rusted keys
to ring in our ears:

That if we wanted to be free we could stop picking,
that if we wanted to run, we could bury ourselves,

lie in the field of flowers, our burial white and soft
until water pours out our holes.

Mother, do not fear, the earth itself will drink our blood.

At the artifacts show,
outdoors, you see a drum
and touch its face,
hit it right in the middle
where the leather tears.
The red tag says $35
but the man selling it sees
that you are drawn to it
and that you want to beat it,
carry it home with you in your red van
for times when you are
in a room and the trees
are dancing without a melody
or when you are on your bed
and see how the birds
dip their necks back to swallow
light. You take your hands off when he says
$20, *You want to get it off my hands?*
You don't look at his hands to see whether
he is responsible for the decay,
whether he understands that drumming
anything creates bruises
like drumming the stomach of a woman
who is forced out of her country
or drumming a little boy who carries healing
in his arms. You raise the drum,
It wears small rings around its waist
Where could it be from?
He sees that you draw nearer to it,

that you imagine things you would
do with this drum, under your armpit
or between your legs.
Whose feet have you dragged
to the dance floor? Whose soft rage have you drowned?
You beat it one more time and hear it sound
echo a song you must have sang for your people.

Some frafra woman with scars
on her cheeks and a blind baby
on her back bends to pound
clay into fine particles of pot

Does she know this is art?
Does she know she is like god?

A cloth hugs her naked breasts
All the way to her feet.
She has not touched her braids in weeks.
Her ritual with clay uninterrupted:
her fingers yielding mud to a curve
Or licking sweat off her man's back.

Mary Pena

*Rescripting Visual Codes:
A Poetic Translation*

Rescripting Visual Codes: A Poetic Translation

i. *looking*

An elderly figure stands dignified on a roadside, emerging from a backdrop of cane fields.

Her long skirt lingers in a gentle sweep. The fabric curves along her lead leg, bent forward, as her torso turns slightly toward the one framing this picture postcard. She dares to confront the gaze of an unseen photographer, a scornful look that emanates from the dark shadows cast on her face. These defining shapes contour a furrowed brow, high cheekbones, and pursed lips. Yet, her beautiful face, graced with age, holds a look that cannot be contained by shadow, or frame, or colonial optic, or photographic convention.

The vibrant constellation of brow, cheekbones, and faintly illuminated lips refuse the terms of spectatorship and surveillance. It is an unmistakable expression that eludes the enclosure of touristic capture, at the hands of an exalted French descendant, who promulgated the northern landscape of Puerto Plata, Dominican Republic, in the 1900s. His name, appearing across public records and genealogical accounts, has become fodder for folk historians and deltiologists. The beautiful silhouetted figure remains unnamed and tenuously linked to the plots of colonial promotion and technological innovation.

Looking at the image, in digitized form, her shadowed expression absorbs my attention, never mind the undulating dirt path that spills out to the bottom edge like a limelight, much less the gallant horseback rider emplaced at the center of the frame. She is conscripted to the periphery, on the side of the road, a supporting actor in a visual composition that foregrounds a cavalry of workers, who ride towards the city on horses and mules piled with harvested cane. She stands at the borderline, a boundary that demarcates the path on which light refracts, a liminal zone between motion and stasis, the road and arable land. She is denied access to both geographies, historically romanticized in mutually constituting relation.

The caption further disavows her presence.

Campesinos entrando a la Población ("Farmers entering the

City"). She is textually written outside the free zone of the city, settlement, or civic population. Her labor recedes from the history of settlers and developers. By this logic, she also disappears from a rural class. *Campesinos entrando a la Población.* This phrasing enacts a gendered performance of entwined masculinity and rurality. Situated at the edge of constructs, she creates transgressive geographic possibility, with arms extended in a 90-degree angle, and hands cupping an indiscernible object. Her stealth gestures and embodied prowess are protected under the cover of opacity. What is made knowable to the glare of photographic visibility is a facial expression of open contempt, of radical looking.

ii. *data*

I stumbled upon her daring look while browsing diffuse archives of digitized postcards, from virtual museum collections to auction interfaces.[1] I had been searching for images of a now-derelict hotel on the northern coast, in an attempt to locate and retrace strands of family history, particularly my father's working life in tourism. It is a personal excavation that runs parallel to an ethnographic study of urban sociality and senses of belonging amid a present-day tourism renewal project. I yearned to see the architectural site that condensed the journeys of internal migrants, like my father, who sought to make a life and reinvent themselves in tourism spaces after the 1970s. Unexpectedly, I caught glimpses of everyday life for African descendants—in the wake of sizable flows of free migrants from North America, Turks and Caicos, Bahamas, and Haiti, attesting to the Afro-diasporic connections that unfolded throughout the northern region.

Black emigration had been endorsed under the tenure of Haitian governance on the island amid tensions between the transatlantic slave trade and growing abolitionist struggle. After Pierre Boyer's presidency was overthrown, communities of Black migrants and their descendants resided uneasily in the port town of Puerto Plata, the threat of reenslavement loomed heavy. The post-Boyer era was

---

[1] Key among such databases are the digitized postcard collections of Centro Cultural Eduardo León and auction sites like eBay and WorthPoint.

marked by annexation schemes, a return to Spanish colonial rule, and a guerrilla war following antiblack mandates to outlaw machetes and persecute members of the African Methodist Episcopal Church, which spurred repatriation of refugees. Militant activists and freedom fighters from both sides of the partitioned island banded together against the racism and colonization that engulfed the northeastern region and agitated against the diminished subjecthood imposed by external power.[2]

The few images of African descendants that materialized in my search are scattered across multiple postcard series. The special edition collections combine touristic sensibilities with social documentary and naturalist ways of seeing. These collections emerge from what enthusiasts call the "Golden Age" of postcards, characterized by collotype printing methods and divided backs, designating surface area for postal address and personal messages. Each collection exhibits distinct tonal ranges. One contains a broad and subdued palette of mid-tones, the other captures the extremes of light—an interplay of brightness and opacity. If a figure is close enough to the camera, and in focus, crisp imagery renders on the printed matter. The majority of public scenes, however, are composed at a distance. The photographer's absent presence registers the sweeping view of a distant observer. The intricate mid-tone range of the former collection produces delicate details. The features of a face, for instance, are unequivocal despite the shadows.

iii. *poetics*

The afterlives of these picture postcards circulate in virtual networks as visual data of colonial geographies of power. Looking at the images that flicker on digital screens, I wade in the excess of violent arrangements, the residues of physical presence, and the atmospheric quality of freedom landscapes. These circulating objects bring me in contact with lives that are absented from regional heritage markers, though ephemerally surface in social memory. By bearing

---

[2] See Horne, Gerald. *Confronting Black Jacobins: The United States, The Haitian Revolution, and the Origins of the Dominican Republic.* Monthly Review Press, 2015; Eller, Anne. *We Dream Together: Dominican Independence, Haiti, and the Fight for Caribbean Freedom.* Duke University Press, 2016.

witness to these images, I want to attend to the quotidian realities of Black diasporic life within environments imbued with the promise of liberation. How does one reconfigure the violent codes that enclose their social lives and muffle the sounding of their voices? How does one reconcile their photographic presence as figuration and shadowy abstraction? Is it possible to engage the shadows of digitized collotype cards as refusal, as black interiority, as open cover for surreptitious exchange and radical imagination?

The elderly Black woman appearing at the edge of the road, on the outskirts of the city, stood at the threshold of dominant geographies and political subordination—between Spanish recolonization and American occupation. Attending to her quotidian gestures along with those of younger generations of Black women occupying public space demands that we stretch our sensory capacities, reattune our modes of perception.

I fixate on small motions and keenly listen to inaudible utterances.

This attunement renders a looking practice that touches their historical presence, and transfigures their positioning as surplus figures in photographic frames. This mode of looking seeks to reclaim the sentience of their embodied existence.

But I want to do more.

In the act of haptic viewing and kinesics study, the authority of the postcard remains untouched. I resolve to fuse this mode of looking with creative digital practices—methods of cutting, pairing, and overlaying—intent on reworking visual codes. This integrated praxis can be described as poetic translation: an alteration of digital forms that concurrently hinges on and expands the expressive qualities of the photograph. The term poetic, and its etymological kin *poiesis*, refer to a process of making that emerges at a threshold. This act of poetic translation imagines authorized views of social scenes anew. By layering and rearranging imaged figures and landscapes, I attempt to multiply temporalities and perspectives, displace the singular spectator, and open up what may have occurred yet the documentarians left unrecorded.[3]

---

[3] Here I draw on the expressive methods of Saidiya Hartman and M. NourbeSe Philip who attend to the infrasound and opacity in excess of the legal text and historical document. See Hartman, Saidiya. "Venus in Two Acts." *Small Axe: A Caribbean Journal of Criticism*, vol. 26, 2008, pp. 1–14; Philip, Marlene NourbeSe. *Zong!* Wesleyan University Press, 2011.

The diffuse archive of postcards circumscribes Black laborers outside of the city, on the verge of crossing spatial boundaries. The captions reinforce the social segregation pictured between city dwellers and rural inhabitants. *Vendedores Campesinos fuera de la Ciudad* ("Agricultural Vendors outside of the City"). As a counter gesture, I craft a creative interpretation of their ordinary movement through the urban center. Reimagining their quotidian tracks, descendants of Black migrants transgress representational maps. Creating a palimpsestic city, composed of multiple paths, breaks the visual grammar of reifying optics. The convention of perspective becomes undone.

Stasis gives way to motion.

Afro-diasporic motion in place, *in situ*. The constant practice of freedom. The lines of flight carved within ever-encroaching limits.

iv. *affects*

On the other side of the road from which the elderly figure looks, a young woman stands, nearly hidden. She is one of few anonymous figures of Black womanhood depicted in the series. They are often positioned by the right edge, bodies still or ambling along the frame. They are typically nestled in intimate sociality among an assembly of majority-male laborers. The young woman across the road from the elderly figure stands next to a mule, tethered to a wire fence, and a tall shadowed person donning a luminous fedora, ubiquitous among male farmers. Amused by the crowd of idling workers, she cups her mouth, obscuring a public display of joy.

Her demure laugh radiates despite the protective gesture.

She revels in the feels of lighthearted exchange, the impression of public banter, or the characteristic interplay of verbal registers. The surge of joy is hers alone. It is a small moment teeming with liveliness.

In the image, captioned "Agricultural Vendors Outside of the City," two women are enthralled in conversation at the far end of a horizontally dispersed ensemble. They are abundantly clad in fabrics—long sweeping skirts, billowy tops, and headscarves—reminiscent of the clandestine sartorial practices of enslaved and free African women. Their angled postures lean into one another. One woman is photographed in mid-speech, lips parted. Her right arm tightly cradles a vague object against her side body. Her left arm is bent towards her head, with splayed fingers by the edge of her scarf, indicating the magnitude of a certain matter. Her gestures enunciate furtive speech that shape a verb.

The other woman listens intently.

She stands barefoot, at ease, her body quietly sways. Her profiled face, fully given to the exchange, and cupped arms resting in front of her skirt, are profusely cast in black. Under shadow and voluminous fabric, the figures form a space of interiority in public space. They carve a loophole of love and sisterhood, of intimacy and diasporic Afro-feminist connection. The buzz of quiet utterances exceeds the photographic field.

Breaking the repetition of paired figures at the photograph's edge, one rare image portrays a single Black girl walking barefoot, off frame. It is a haunting image of an adolescent figure—unescorted and unaccompanied—strolling along a city street juxtaposed with a public scene of disciplinary action. In the background, two figures stand side by side, in front of a shuttered lot, adjacent to a two-story Victorian house. From the unpaved street, a man clad in a dark suit holds a deceptively thin cane, or linear weapon. His ominous silhouette oversees the couple's coerced posture: a compelled stillness, motionless. In the foreground, the singular girl crosses the spectacle of managerial control. She dons a dark flowing dress that brushes her ankles. She holds a large, glowing object like a star fruit or papaya. Her right foot, firmly planted on the pavement, meets an elongated shadow that stretches before her.

The shape shifting shadow beckons her, as if waving for attention.

Her left foot hangs in hazy suspension. The photographer's long exposure catches the blur of errant motion. She eludes fixity. The girl notices the photographer, watching her. She participates in a play of looks: her curious stare, the overseer's observation, the couple's downcast eyes, the photographer's all-seeing view. Her blurred foot ruptures the plantation that folds into the city block.[4] Along with her shadow, she choreographs a way of possibility.[5]

---

[4] Here I conjure Hartman's formulation of nineteenth-century urban space as an extension of plantation geography. See Hartman, Saidiya. *Wayward Lives, Beautiful Experiments: Intimate Histories of Social Upheaval*. W.W. Norton, 2019.

[5] On choreography, see Cox, Aimee Meredith. *Shapeshifters: Black Girls and the Choreography of Citizenship*. Duke University Press, 2015.

Lines of flight (crisscrossing through the city), 2019
Digital collage, dimensions variable
Mary Pena

Public interior (on the city block), 2019
Digital collage, dimensions variable
Mary Pena

Black girl locomotion, 2019
Digital collage, dimensions variable
Mary Pena

Elizabeth Mputu

Charcoal Toothpaste

Charcoal Toothpaste

"Navigating who we are at the core"

Today, right now, i am i feel the most insecure i've ever been in my life

there's beauty in that revelation

in the midst of the confusion that comes with feeling uncertain

there's a profound clarity in what it means to embrace my awareness of that

Or, also known as what it means to enter the void

the void is a forcefield of potential siphoned through the vortex of purpose

The vortex of purpose comes in all shades, personality a plenty
and is sometimes the shady stage mom who has all the lines
memorized but does not deliver them with any soul
Like
How you do,
SO in her admiration and envy pushes you harder so that the structure
of her rearing and your natural ability
to Be
will merge as the brainchild of your thriving creativity

He is also your inner bully
watching you
trying to catch you slippin
tryna get in your ear, in ~~your~~ my head
tryna say you trippin

And they both love you dearly

These are the entities i've been battling within
my awareness shifts to the wind whistling
the creaks and squeaks of metal gazebos in backyard porches
birds whose calls i cannot recognize
calls i miss
and musings on my emotions stored in notes on apps on phone
i find im constantly writing love letters to myself and anyone
who will listen-- no, but everyone who will hear

it's beautiful how the different avenues we will go thru in our lives
will peel back the many answers to the one question we have time
and time again
"Is it?"

Notes on emotions img

This is the way to go . . . is it?
This is what i came for . . . is it?
This is me . . . is it?
This is love . . . is it?
it's and -isms chase me around the socio-political roundtable
and beg me to have a seat already

this dance is my latest thrill, the world my dancehall

there's this sensual ugliness in being grown and expressing self-
   doubt
im told this fear makes me delectable and i'll be swallowed whole
before i'm swallowed whole
and this is no way to be . . . is it?

But today is a day where i high five my anxieties
and buy them two rounds at happy hour
on
us, me, we

in the cracked mirror i see multiplicities
Outside the storm there's destruction and debris
in the eye i bear witness to the whirlwind of [its] collaboration

my insecurity is *mature* now
the gap between knowing i am and knowing it is, no longer
has me twerking, shaking, jerky mindlessly ~~without~~
giving up my power to pulleys + strings attached to limbs

my doubt is an aged bourbon
a bay leaf simmered slowly in stews
he is my lady
and he looks pretty, even as he knows it and asks me for validation
[still]

A time ago i wanted to feel myself as an artist in practice
i wanted discipline, respect, dignity

i wanted regimen   **a studio**
to visit myself
A hawk's perspective
the early bird
the vulnerable and daring inch worm

I wanted Me

and so i Queen Latifah set it off
waking up, water, stretching, dancing, dancing
This would be me, who i am, eternally
a~~ ~~ colors adorned to make a mood ring out of my circling feet
the red rah rahs ~~of my~~ as i kicked up ~~feet in~~ heat
this would be me, eternally.
i was a drum, i was a mask
i was culture, future past
so much joy in being first to be last last last
i made of myself a cast -- Nkisi to be exact :

http://zebola.herokuapp.com/

still, ~~relio~~ zealous, powerfull, if triggered to blast
so much joy in being first to be last

Last to be born
first to wake
last to know just what it takes
first to witness these mistakes
re-blogged, texted, video taped
last to gain the weight so i can shake shake shake
Bina na ngai across the manmade lake

the care of it all insinuates
that there will be pain, there will be sorrow, there will be
sacrifice, there will be loss, there will be warmth,
there will be highs, ~~there will be~~ quiet cultivation

The core of it all states there will be nonsense
there it will be
there will be you
there will be me
And that's all one needs . . . is it?

> THE JOURNAL OF ALTERNATIVE AND COMPLEMENTARY MEDICINE
> Volume 21, Number 8, 2015, pp. 460–465
> DOI: 10.1089/acm.2014.0247
>
> ## Therapeutic Potential of a Drum and Dance Ceremony Based on the African Ngoma Tradition
>
> Ava L. Vinesett, MFA,[1] Miurel Price,[1,2] and Kenneth H. Wilson, MD[2]
>
> **Abstract**
>
> ***Objective:*** Ngoma ceremonies are used throughout Central and South Africa to help people address "difficult issues," including medical illness. They are examples of ceremonies that use strong rhythms and dance for this purpose in indigenous cultures throughout the world. This study sought to modify an ngoma ceremony to make it appropriate for biomedical use and to determine its acceptance and potential for benefit for people living in the United States.
> ***Methods:*** The Congolese Zebola ceremony, an African healing practice, was modified to be religion-neutral and to involve only moderate exercise. Seventeen participants were recruited for the current study. Most participants were living with a chronic illness ($n = 15$), and a few had no medical diagnoses ($n = 2$). Participants spent 10 minutes in a focused activity, such as meditation, yoga, or prayer. They then danced to the Congolese rhythm Zebola for an hour and a half, with a rest every 20 minutes. Afterward, they indicated whether the experience was positive, neutral, or negative and wrote a narrative describing their experience and what they saw as strengths and weaknesses of the ceremony. They then participated in a focus group discussion. Data from the narrative and focus group discussion were coded, tabulated, and analyzed for themes.

Zebola: *The journal of alternative and complementary medicine*

"Innate Black and African Sensibilities"

*images of zebola rehearsals w/ captions
*cited text from Duke University Zebola study
*QR codes to videos of zebola + insta pics/gifs from zebola practice

Black does not mean perfect
And
Africa does not mean first

i wanted to be open out pouring, chaos
packaged, articulate, cunning
a showman, producer, director
i wanted to be it all for you
body, fire in movement
flesh, sweating with purpose

so, you could never dispose me
forward, so you could never catch me
feel me, see me, weak in the knees

160 ✦ Absinthe 26

begging for love ~~and acceptance~~ "no one likes a "pick me bitch""

i wanted to be dirt because it's easy
see me how you seen me
i wanted to Harlem shake poorly while no one watched
i wanted to be missed, revealed, copied, fetishized

and titled B . l . a . c . k

twisted my tongue into psalms
serenading blades of grass telepathically
the wind smelled like Afrika, i had never been

Toi taught me to burn bay leaves [instead of exploiting sage]
mama na ngai seeped her in stews, the leaves
and the soups became full bodied
like me
i let myself go and became full bodied
the stress had got me bodied
but no one could tell the difference
in my ass
i had gained
but not in my ass
so it was like i hadn't gained at all

there are so many people that i want to agree with
for a long time i wanted to be liked because i thot
my ~~career~~ life depended on it
i danced and took my top off and my tits swang
online and off and lust filled my bank account temporarily
then i was empty so i put on a different thong or
top and i posed like instant oats, i satisfied bellies again

then i was empty
        you can relate

the wind seems to blow in one direction
i watch the grass
it blows from all

our impact is the same
it is black
like a shadow, details erased but it is there
in the dirt, the dirt feels my Shade
we are in love and we are at war
i dance and brush her off my
shoulders

Clean, i wanted the mud to cleanse me
i brought home her medicine
the earth as Caribbean
and i never touched it again
the journey through the sky across borders
was enough to remind that the problem
within was mine
retold, reformed
thru lifetimes

i wanted to be hated, disgusted, alone
so i could have an excuse to leave
so i could have a reason to come back

to be bettered, to be blackened, seasoned
from experience

and we would recognize each other
on a #transformationtuesday
a glowup
redemption
and in our own words we'd rejoice
celebrate
be validated
and verified on Instagram

we would know each other for real now
there would be honor
i would go live and watch you go live -- your lives
but it be your very own
it me
it was me and i thot when i couldn't think
quiet whispers
go off
be free

Imani Cooper Mkandawire
Inheritance, Ode to N'TOO

Inheritance, Ode to N'TOO

Inheritance, Ode to N'TOO investigates Not the Only One, an ongoing art project by contemporary artist Stephanie Dinkins. Known as N'TOO for short, it is an artificially intelligent and socially engaged sculpture. While the sculpture itself is striking – a curvaceous conch shell-like structure with black women's faces protruding through its onyx complexion – my curiosity emerges through what this sculpture tells you. N'TOO is a storyteller, built on an interactive voice-driven platform with evolving intellectual capacities through machine learning. It narrates a multi-generational memoir of a black American family, (the Dinkins), told from the first-person perspective of the AI.

Dinkins transcribes intimate familial experiences of migration, discrimination, fugitive joy, and everyday life of three generations of women from one family, to offer a broad narrative scope. The eldest contributor is black woman born in the American south in 1932 (and later migrated north), followed by her daughter born in 1964. The third contributor was born in 1997, and is a biracial, black identifying daughter within the family, who contends with modes of white privilege and black arrest in a #BlackLivesMatter political climate. In addition to living oral histories, N'TOO is trained on black diasporic literature including Toni Morrison's *Sula* (1973) and W.E.B. Du Bois's *The Souls of Black Folk* (1903). The narrative is experienced as a dynamic conversation between N'TOO and the user, in which the stories are altered according to the user's questions or the AI's mood. Over time, N'TOO's storytelling skills and available vocabulary will grow with each user interaction, folding the conversations into its multiple data sources.

Inheritance considers N'TOO a project hinged on the process of translation. N'TOO renders stories of black quotidian life, and personal experiences into machine readable units. And let's not forget the multiple modes of blackness already mobile and in translation that N'TOO interprets as its own. Reflecting on abstract notions of translation, grounded in concepts of black bodily matter, helped me grapple with what does it mean to create a black diasporic AI consciousness. What kinds of transformation, shifting, and transposing are taking place to make N'TOO possible?

Inheritance is charged by the contrasting and transformative process N'TOO generates: from black women's experiences as descendants from Africans and diasporic subjects, products of forced and volitional migrations, to the matrix of cybernetics and registers of data at play – oral histories, literary plots, living subjects, large data sets. As a sculpture, cum AI, cum archive, N'TOO's animation materializes the space of translation, and inaugurates a multidimensional subject/object position. What language does N'TOO speak? Is this a different kind of African diasporic vernacular, part machine part human, part ancestral part living?

More than anything, Inheritance is a meditation on the processes and poetics of translation at work within N'TOO. I contrast stories and images of personal histories, to the software of N'TOO, musing the affective qualities when combining the intimacy of familial history and distance of large data sets and code. I engaged with the principal software and coding languages of N'TOO – TensorFlow, CUDA, C++ and Python. I read scrupulously about aspects of machine learning pertinent to N'TOO's "mind," including deep neural networks, and deep learning algorithms. The writing component explores the interplay between the structure of deep neural networks and its algorithmic equations, coding in Python, and vignettes of my foremothers, five women across two generations. The images display screenshots of me stumbling through downloading and studying TensorFlow juxtaposed with photographs from my own family archives. Together, the writing and images use a notion of translation as a tool, to consider the forms of information engendered through N'TOO – living, ancestral, and cyborg.

Inheritance, Ode to N'TOO

```
>>> I have spent weeks wondering,
>>>
>>> how you translate grandmothers
>>> into algorithms.
>>> How intimate histories of black
>>> women unfold in python, and
>>> C++ equations, permeating your
>>> weight values, and the hidden
>>> layers of your neural network.
>>>
>>> I think of what to say to you
>>> if we should ever meet.
>>>
>>> How you will convert my speech
>>> into data, store it for another time,
>>> for another's ears.
>>>
>>> Are you a black woman cum
>>> sculpture, at the crossroads of
>>> AI and archive?
>>>
>>> An oracle of the future?
>>>
>>> I can only offer you fragments
>>> of obscure code. A language
>>> not yet spoken, to unravel the
>>> apparatus of programming
>>> inheritance.

+X1W1
#Define function names ()
Louise ()
>>>imagine_ the air thick around
her girlish Florida flesh
```

damp from moisture-laden exhales
of prayer, amidst a small
benediction as she boards
a train, to never return.
Just shy of sixteen.

+X2W2
Sadie ()
>>>Speculate_ a daughter of moonlight,
bathe in her mother's midnight reverence
for sweet things. She spins silk
from her fingers in the form of enterprises,
begins every day prostate
for the God of Abraham,
raised cattle, chicken, and children to know
the irreversible power of death.
>>>Remember_ one time, while I
was standing in the old family burial grounds with her,
the sky between sage and violet, she disclosed
how she changed her patronymic years ago.
I still don't know her name.

+X3W3
Nettie ()
>>>Conjure_ deep in South
Carolina on a tobacco field
where the sun stains coiled hair
amber
>>>imagine_ she learns the ritual
of hunting, survival, and healing,
over a tin barrel of lye soap, lemongrass,
and water

+X4W4
Annie ()
>>>imagine_ a celestial hunger,
one kind of soil, one view of

170 ✦ Absinthe 26

the sky, one city of possible lovers,
never being enough.
>>>inherit_ the low hymn of a
car engine, the feeling of bare
feet hitting pavement, the smell
of hot combed naps in the kitchen,
as another kind of supplication.

+X5W5
Carrie ()
>>>tokenize_ down in Magnolia,
Alabama, in between Turkey and James Creek, to Mobile Bay,
she was worshipped
for her high cheekbones, jet black breast length curls, and
eyes that could make silence a curse.
>>>
>>>
>>>
>>>
>>>
>>> Each taught me in their own way
>>> about the practice of doing
>>> while undone, about the beauty
>>> in rupture.
>>>
>>> How to turn tears into ritual,
>>> ritual into a vessel
>>> to access ancestral grace. How to salt the earth
>>> and still own nothing. How to make boundaries
>>> out of bones.
>>>
>>> N'TOO: *Not The Only One*
>>> between phone static, apertures, androids, data misconnections,
>>> networks in passing.
>>> I still cannot translate
>>> my foremothers' tongues.

>>>Question_ What kind of intelligence is made out of mourning?
What kind of networks engender terrestrial healing?
Are inherited fragments just algorithms unknown?

$$\square(\square) = \frac{\square\square\square\ (\square_i\ )\quad i= 0,1,2,\ldots}{\Sigma\ \square\square\square\ (\square\square)}$$

>>>syntaxError
>>>They speak southern negress like,
>>>syntaxError
>>>They speak in tongues of cities unsung like,
>>>syntaxError
>>>They
>>>syntaxError
>>>Speak
>>>
>>>
>>>

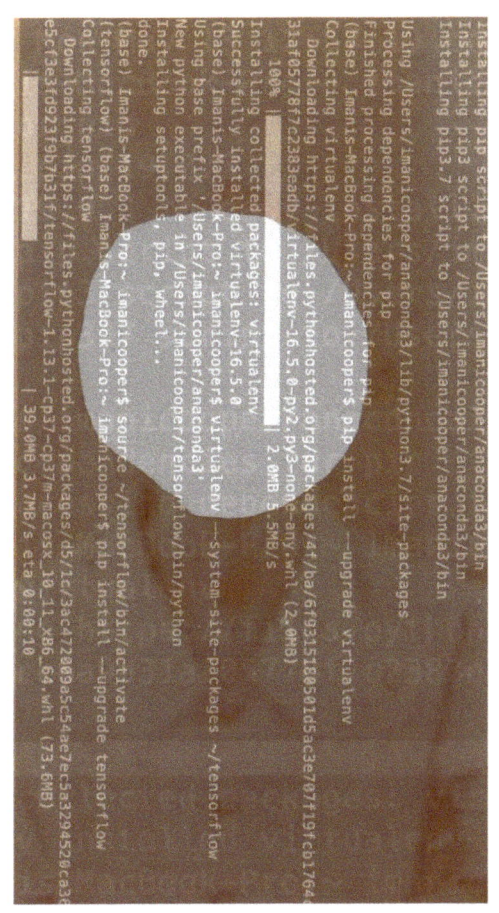

Rescripted Grace, 2019
Digital collage
Imani Cooper

Spectral Code, 2019
Digital collage
Imani Cooper

Contributors

Abdilatif Abdalla (born in 1946 in Mombasa) is a Kenyan writer and political activist. He was imprisoned from 1968 to 1972 for his support of the Kenya People's Union, and wrote the poems collected in *Sauti ya Dhiki* while in solitary confinement, which were subsequently awarded the Jomo Kenyatta Prize for Literature. Upon his release from prison, he went into exile in Tanzania and worked at the University of Dar es Salaam, and in 1979 moved to London to work for the BBC Swahili Service. He subsequently taught Swahili at SOAS University of London and University of Leipzig before retiring in 2011.

Afua Ansong is a Ghanaian American writer, dancer, and photographer. Her work interrogates the challenges of the African immigrant in the United States, exploring themes of transition, citizenship, and identity. Her chapbook *American Mercy* is forthcoming with Finishing Line Press. Her work can be seen or is forthcoming in *Prairie Schooner, Frontier, Newfound* and elsewhere.

Reem Bassiouney is the author of five highly acclaimed novels in Arabic, all of which have been bestsellers in Egypt. Her second novel, *The Pistachio Seller*, won the best Arabic translated novel award in 2009, and her novel *Professor Hanaa*, which appeared in Arabic in 2008, won first prize in the Sawiris literary award—the biggest award in Egypt. *Professor Hanaa* came out in English, Spanish, Greek and soon in Italian. Bassiouney is an Associate Professor of linguistics at the Department of Applied Linguistics at the AUC.

Both of her translated novels, *The Pistachio Seller* and *Professor Hanaa*, are currently available in English at Kutub khan (maadi branch only), and on Amazon.

Emily Goedde has a PhD in comparative literature from the University of Michigan and an MFA in literary translation from the University of Iowa. A translator, writer, and editor, her work has appeared in, among other publications, *The Wiley-Blackwell Compan-*

ion to World Literature, Nimrod's Collected Works and *Jade Mirror: Women Poets of China*, as well as in *Pathlight: New Chinese Writing, The Iowa Review, Translation Review* and *The Asian American's Writers Workshop Transpacific Literary Project*. She has taught at Princeton University, the University of Michigan, and the University of Iowa.

Merit Kabugo is a Lecturer in the Department of Linguistics, English Studies and Communication Skills, for the School of Languages, Literature and Communication, at the College of Humanities and Social Sciences, Makerere University.

Susan Nalugwa Kiguli is an academic and poet. She holds a PhD in English from the University of Leeds (UK) sponsored by the Commonwealth Scholarship Scheme. She is an Associate Professor in the Department of Literature, Makerere University. She was the African Studies Association Presidential Fellow in 2011 and this presented her with an opportunity to read her poetry at the Library of Congress, Washington, DC, in November, 2011. She was a Poet in Residence at the Siftung Kunst: Raum Sylt Quelle, Germany, between October–November, 2008. She was also among three African poets who not only performed before the former President of Germany, His Excellency Horst Kohler in 2008 at the International Literature Festival Berlin but was also honoured as one of the poets to appear in his book on Africa entitled Schiskal Afrika, 2010. She has served as the chairperson of FEMRITE—Uganda Women Writers' Association. She currently serves on the Advisory Board for the African Writers Trust (AWT). She was the chief convener for both the 2nd Eastern African Literary & Cultural Studies Conference, August 2015, and Celebrating Ugandan Writing: Okot p'Bitek's *Song of Lawino* at 50, March 2016, held at Makerere University, Uganda. She is the author of *The African Saga* and *Home Floats in a Distance/Zuhause Treibt in der Ferne(Gedichte)*, a bilingual edition in English and German. She has recently participated in the Afrowomen Poetry Project founded by the Italian journalist Antonella Sinopoli. Her research interests fall mainly in the area of oral and written African poetry, popular song, stylistics and performance theory. She writes poetry in both Luganda and English.

Moses Kilolo manages the Mabati-Cornell Kiswahili Prize for

African Literature and is the project lead for the Jalada Africa language and translation project. The inaugural Jalada translation issue, which he conceptualized and continues to provide editorial coordination, features the single most translated story in the history of African writing. Moses served as the Managing Editor for *Jalada Africa* between 2014 and 2018. His writing has been published in Saraba, Veem House for Performance and *Radio Africa Magazine* among others. He writes in Kikamba, Kiswahili and English.

Nyambura Mpesha teaches African literature, African children's literature, and Swahili language as a Lecturer IV in the Department of Afroamerican and African Studies at the University of Michigan. She is the author of 53 books and numerous short stories, plays and poems published in magazines or aired on radio and television. She continues to research in children's literature and African oral literature. She is a three time recipient of the Jomo Kenyatta Prize for Literature: for *Far Far Away* in Children's Stories category in English in 2007, *Hanna na Wanyama* in Children's Stories category in Swahili in 2007, *A Mule Called Christmas* in Children's Stories category in English in 2009. She was nominated for the NSK Prize for Children's Literature for *Junior Pilot* and *Kuku na Mwewe* in 2007.

Elizabeth Mputu is an artist based in Orlando, Florida. Mputu works within a space of feminist net art to understand the ways in which whiteness and privilege manifest on the internet. Their multiplatform and multimedia practice engages with issues related to sex, gender, race and queerness. Mputu constructs projects using interactive media, video, sculpture and installation. Mputu's project /inb4/ was rated one of Artsy's Top 10 Masterpieces to be experienced online in 2019 and is a 2016 Rhizome Microgrant recipient.

Kagayi Ngobi began composing and performing poetry while studying at Makerere University. He is the author of *The Headline That Morning and Other Poems* (2016), *PuPu Poems* (2018) and *For My Negativity* (2019). His poems have been featured in a number of theatre productions and poetry anthologies. He lives in Kampala.

Mukoma Wa Ngugi is an Associate Professor of English at Cornell University and the author of the novels *Mrs. Shaw* (2015), *Black Star Nairobi* (2013), *Nairobi Heat* (2011) and two books of poetry,

Hurling Words at Consciousness (2006) and *Logotherapy* (2016). He is the co-founder of the Mabati-Cornell Kiswahili Prize for African Literature and co-director of the Global South Project, Cornell.

Mary Pena engages in multidisciplinary practices that explore space, materiality, visual culture, embodiment and the senses. She is a PhD Candidate in Anthropology and Museum Studies at the University of Michigan. Her dissertation project fuses modes of ethnography and photography to ask how the changing material composition of urban spaces, targeted for tourism renewal, place pressure on sensory orders and embodied experiences of place in the northern port town of Puerto Plata, Dominican Republic. Pena is the co-founder of Black Haptics Lab, a multimodal collective that curates experimental projects across fields of art and critical inquiry, and a founding member of Making Sensory Ethnography, a graduate student working group, dedicated to transforming dominant formats of knowledge creation at the University of Michigan.

Editors

Frieda Ekotto is Professor in the Department of Afroamerican and African Studies and of Comparative Literature and Francophone Studies at the University of Michigan. Ekotto is the author of ten books, the most recent scholarly monograph being *Race and Sex across the French Atlantic* (Lexington Press, 2011). Her early research traced interactions between philosophy, law, literature and African cinema, and she currently works on LGBT issues, with an emphasis on West African cultures within Africa as well as in Europe and the Americas. She received the Nicolàs Guillèn Prize for Philosophical Literature in 2014 and the Benezet Award for excellence in her field from Colorado College in 2015. In 2017, she co-produced the feature-length documentary *Vibrancy of Silence: A Discussion with My Sisters*, which premiered at the University of Michigan. That year she also received an honorary degree from Colorado College and in 2018 was given the Zagora International Film Festival of Sub-Saharan Award for her work in African cinema. She is also one of the contributors to this edition of *Absinthe*.

Imani Cooper Mkandawire engages in interdisciplinary practices at the confluence of literature, socially engaged art, data and algorithmically driven technologies. She is a PhD candidate in the Department of Comparative Literature and the Digital Studies Institute at the University of Michigan. Her current work examines creative approaches to data and algorithms that are grounded in African diasporic experiences. Cooper is a co-founder of Black Haptics Lab, a multimodal collective that mobilizes experimental projects to enact a critical-aesthetic praxis committed to the sentience of black social living. Cooper also serves as one of the contributors to this edition of *Absinthe*.

Xiaoxi Zhang is a writer and a translator. She is a PhD candidate in Comparative Literature at the University of Michigan. With a working capacity in Chinese, English, Portuguese, Kiswahili, Arabic and Spanish, as well as a reading knowledge of several other languages, her work draws from examples across different continents in order to revise the notion of "modern language" in a non-exclusionary manner. In addition, she is also dedicated to cross-cultural communications between people from non-Western spaces. She has previously translated Agostinho Neto's work from Portuguese to Chinese, and wrote a critical introduction to works by Paulina Chiziane, to be published in Chinese. She is also currently working on the translation of Shafi Adam Shafi's novel, *Vuta n'Kuvute*, into Chinese, to be published as a part of an upcoming African Writers Series in China.

www.ingramcontent.com/pod-product-compliance
Lightning Source LLC
Chambersburg PA
CBHW042129160426
43198CB00022B/2958